'Jelena has done a brilliant job in showing how coaches and trainers can partner most effectively with the latest generations of A.I. in ways that give greater benefits to the coachee's and learners. Essential reading for all coaches, trainers and those in the human development professions.'

Professor Peter Hawkins, *Best-selling author and global thought leader in leadership, coaching and organizational development*

'*Partnering with AI in Coaching and Human Skills Development* is at the forefront of the implementation of AI in human society. In this work, looking through a humanistic constructivist lens at how AI can be used, it moves the conversation from what is inside the AI and how does is work to how is it used most effectively.'

Joel DiGirolamo, *Vice President of Research and Data Science, International Coaching Federation*

'*Partnering with AI in Coaching and Human Skills Development* is a must-read for coaches, educators, leaders, and anyone looking to harness Generative AI for human growth. Jelena Pavlović offers a practical guide to integrating AI as a powerful partner in human skill development—timely, insightful, and essential for the AI era.'

Dr Dragan Gašević, *Distinguished Professor of Learning Analytics at Monash University, Faculty of Information Technology and Director of the Centre for Learning analytics at Monash University*

'*Groundbreaking and insightful, Partnering with AI in Coaching and Human Skills Development* is a must-read for anyone navigating the complex intersection between AI and human growth. The book blends research, real-world applications and practical guidance in order to offer a useful roadmap for leveraging AI for the advancement of coaching and, more broadly, for skills development.'

Dr Vlad Glaveanu, *Full Professor of Psychology, School of Psychology, Dublin City University, Director, DCU Centre for Possibility Studies, Adjunct Professor, Centre for the Science of Learning and Technology, University of Bergen*

'In this groundbreaking book, Jelena Pavlović, an authority on coaching from a constructivist perspective, shows how this approach can incorporate AI as an active partner. It not only provides a theoretical and research background but also numerous engaging exercises to guide readers' experimentation with AI.'

David Winter, *Professor Emeritus of Clinical Psychology, University of Hertfordshire, UK*

'This book stands out for its practical guidance on leveraging AI to enhance human potential. While it focuses on coaching and skill development, its approach to building AI agents offers a versatile framework that can be applied across various domains. A must-read for innovators in technology and beyond.'

Jan Dolinaj, *CTO, Levi9*

'*Partnering with AI in Coaching and Human Skills Development* by Jelena Pavlović is a groundbreaking exploration of the intersection between artificial intelligence and human development. This book offers a comprehensive and insightful guide for coaches, educators, and professionals seeking to harness the power of AI to enhance their practice. This book is not just a theoretical but a practical guide that empowers readers to become co-creators with AI. By offering step-by-step instructions for customizing AI agents, Pavlović ensures that readers can apply the concepts to their unique contexts and professional needs.'

Milan Gospić, *Microsoft Garage Serbia Lead*

'Dr Pavlović does an excellent job at holding the hand of the reader through the possibility of partnering with AI, ultimately boosting our impact and reach as coaches. As we accelerate towards unchartered territories at an incredible speed, I'd definitely recommend this book to rationalize, comprehend and appreciate that the path to partnering with AI is an immense resource for our profession.'

Gabriele Galassi, *Chartered Psychologist, Head of L&D and Social Impact at Mollie*

'AI is now a highly debated topic in every area of our lives, including coaching. This book presents a compelling constructivist approach, demonstrating how AI can support and enhance coaching rather than replace human expertise.'

Dorota Joanna Bourne, *Professor of Leadership and Change Management, Henley Business School, UK*

Partnering with AI in Coaching and Human Skills Development

Partnering with AI in Coaching and Human Skills Development explores the transformative impact of artificial intelligence (AI) on coaching practices and, more broadly, on learning and development.

This book presents insights on the integration of AI in coaching, coach training, mentoring, supervision, and more, highlighting its potential to augment the human side of learning and development. Providing practical insights, real-world examples, and actionable strategies for integrating AI into coaching practices, the author addresses the growing interest in AI-augmented learning and development (L&D) solutions and fills a significant gap, highlighting topics such as human-AI collaboration, co-evolving with AI, and organizational perspectives of AI.

Drawing on the real-world case studies, cutting-edge research, and practical insights, this book provides a comprehensive guide for human resources professionals, executive coaches, L&D experts, organizational leaders, and AI enthusiasts seeking to leverage AI in their work.

Jelena Pavlović is Associate Professor of Organizational Development and Change at the University of Belgrade and founder and CEO of Koucing centar. With a background in psychology and extensive experience in coaching, Jelena has published numerous academic papers and books on coaching and L&D. Her recent research focuses on the potential of AI to augment the human side of coaching and coach training. Jelena has a unique blend of expertise in coaching and practical applications of AI-augmented L&D.

Partnering with AI in Coaching and Human Skills Development

A Constructivist Guidebook for Innovation

Jelena Pavlović

Routledge
Taylor & Francis Group

LONDON AND NEW YORK

Designed cover image: Getty Images

First published 2026
by Routledge
4 Park Square, Milton Park, Abingdon, Oxon OX14 4RN

and by Routledge
605 Third Avenue, New York, NY 10158

Routledge is an imprint of the Taylor & Francis Group, an informa business

© 2026 Jelena Pavlović

British Library Cataloguing-in-Publication Data
A catalogue record for this book is available from the British Library

Library of Congress Cataloging-in-Publication Data
A catalog record has been requested for this book

ISBN: 978-1-032-95088-4 (hbk)
ISBN: 978-1-032-95085-3 (pbk)
ISBN: 978-1-003-58314-1 (ebk)

DOI: 10.4324/9781003583141

Typeset in Times New Roman
by Taylor & Francis Books

To my family, Jakša, Janko, and Jugoslav

Contents

Figure

Tables

Boxes

Acknowledgements

This research was financially supported by the Ministry of Science, technological development and innovation of the Republic of Serbia, as part of the project of University of Belgrade – Faculty of Philosophy (contract number: ugovora 451–03–66/2024–03/ 200163).

Project Coachia was financed by the Innovation Fund from the European Union Pre-Accession Assistance and from the budget of the Republic of Serbia, the line of the Ministry of Science, Technological Development and Innovation.

Foreword

Artificial intelligence (AI) is in the news every day. Its time has come. Recently AI has started to be used within the coaching field. This book, *Partnering with AI in Coaching and Human Skills Development* by Professor Jelena Pavlović, explores the integration of AI into the domains of coaching and human skills development. The approach taken is grounded in constructivist psychology principles, emphasising the active role of people in constructing meaning and identity through experience and reflection. A comprehensive framework is presented for how AI can be a collaborative partner, enhancing the learning and development processes through AI agents such as AI Tutors, Simulators, Coaches, Mentors, and Reflection Buddies. These agents are designed to support users in goal setting, experimentation, reflection, and learning through personalised and contextually relevant interactions.

The book examines the practical applications of AI in various domains, highlighting the potential of AI to transform traditional coaching and educational practices. Through case studies, such as the development and deployment of Coachia, an AI system for human skills development, Professor Pavlović shares how AI can provide feedback within safe practice environments. She also addresses the challenges of integrating AI into professional practice, highlighting the importance of ethical concerns, ongoing research, and user-driven innovation to ensure that AI remains aligned with human values and goals. By combining psychological frameworks, AI capabilities, and user feedback, the book provides a road map for both individual and organisational growth.

This cutting-edge book is an excellent resource for coaches, educators, psychologists, and professionals looking to channel the power of AI in their practice.

Dr Stephen Palmer, PhD
Director, National Academy of Coaching Psychology

Introduction

AI as everyone's partner

A couple of (non-futuristic) scenarios

Imagine you run a training program. You have an artificial intelligence (AI) Companion that helps you create the curriculum, continuously collect feedback from learners, adapt the training approach in each session based on learners' and AI feedback. Your AI Companion helps you understand the social interaction in the classroom, pedagogical approach, and the overall value of your training program. Even if you are a highly experienced and expert-level educator, your AI Companion sheds light on some of the "blind spots," helps you reflect on your approach and practice. And you become inspired to try out new approaches and bring even greater value to your learners.

Now imagine you are a coach. You know your methodologies well; almost nothing can surprise you. You get your AI Coach as an add to your coaching practice. It works alongside you between your sessions with the clients. Clients have access to support almost whenever they need it. The AI Coach works in line with what you consider to be excellence in coaching. It can adapt its style and methodologies. It can adopt the general approach of partnering in coaching and co-creating the process with the client. Clients come to sessions with you with insights from their AI Coach. You continue and learn that there is a new quality in the process with AI augmentation.

Imagine you are an organizational professional working in the domain of learning and development. You are planning a new leadership development program for your colleagues. You can use AI Tutors, human coaches, AI Team coaches, immersive virtual reality (VR) environments based on AI. Choice of different human, AI, or hybrid interventions make you feel empowered and creative in your work.

You are a novice coach. You enter a coach training program. Alongside your human trainers, you have an AI Tutor to help you explain coaching concepts. Once you are ready to start practicing, you have your AI Mentor who can assist you in providing formative feedback to your sessions, before you submit them to your human mentor. You have an AI Reflective Buddy

DOI: 10.4324/9781003583141-1

that helps you capture transformative moments on your learning journey and test new approaches in your emerging practice.

Or you are an organizational leader. You want to improve your skills in leading difficult performance conversations. Together with your human trainers, you have an AI Simulator that helps you practice. It provides relevant scenarios, plays the role you assign to it, and provides you feedback. Your AI Simulator helps you learn about your strengths and about what you can improve as a leader. It gives you a sense of ease in learning and development.

From developing minds to developing machines (that develop minds): Are we all developers now?

All these scenarios are about what is possible now with generative artificial intelligence (GenAI). And almost all of the AI agents mentioned above (except for the VR environment perhaps) coaches and educators can build now. They don't need coding knowledge. They don't need technical infrastructure. This book is about how to build your own AI agents in coaching and human skills development.

This book also invites coaches and educators to think of themselves as no-code developers. We are all developers now. We shape the interaction with GenAI to create meaningful AI outputs that were impossible previously without hours of coding and technical knowledge. GenAI has emerged as a general-purpose technology. In this book it is framed as a general-purpose technology for human skills development. Although these tools can transform learning, they require thoughtful design to align with humanistic values and ethical considerations.

What this means is that coaches and educators are becoming users of GenAI in their domains. With their unique knowledge of their fields of expertise, coaches and educator are best positioned to design AI learning experiences, evaluate them, and improve. In a sense, coaches and educators are becoming developers now – developers of minds and machines.

AI as organizational partner: Embedded, hybrid, highly customized AI development

Organizational learning benefits hugely. A typical employee has many more opportunities to learn and grow. As it was once democratizing and liberating to go to various massive open online courses and learn whatever you needed, now it is becoming even more tailored to you. Custom AI Tutors and simulators help you achieve your own goals, when you need it and how it's most convenient to you.

For organizations, bringing AI as a partner to learning and development (L&D) departments brings many benefits (DiGirolamo, 2024; Norton et al., 2024). Perhaps most important, AI as organizational L&D partner makes learning embedded into daily work practices. Employees may turn to AI solutions to find information, practice skills, and get feedback. Work and education don't divide. The human and social aspects of L&D are still there. AI comes to augment these.

Everyone gets a new partner in development

With current AI capabilities everyone can get an AI Coach, Tutor, Mentor, Simulator, a Buddy for reflection, and more. Online coaching platforms made a promise of democratizing coaching a decade ago. With GenAI, human skills development is even more accessible. Ways of developing become more creative. And we all have a part to play.

Developers get partners in coaches and educators

No-code approach to technology may shift the mindset of many classic developers. They may learn that developing AI is even more effective if human developers are alongside. Coaches and educators know how to coach AI. And GenAI at its current stage of development is highly coachable. These new work teams may be an important driver of GenAI development across domains.

What can you find inside this book

This book is about how we can all make use of GenAI to develop. The book is about how AI can be a partner in development. For coaches and educators, it is getting a useful new co-worker. For organizations, it is about getting a new type of provider that revolutionizes the field of L&D. For AI developers, it is about psychological principles of working with and designing AI. For everyone, it is a journey of what is possible with GenAI that helps us on various learning and development paths.

In Chapter 1 the constructivist approach is introduced as psychology of how to partner with AI. The constructivist approach accounts for complexity in human-AI collaboration. It talks about mutual meaning-making, lack of one final (human or AI) "truth," and about the importance of negotiating meaning between humans and AI. The constructivist approach draws our attention on how we become a part of what emerges as GenAI reality. It calls for constant reflection on what goals we are setting with AI and how we are achieving those goals. It also calls for AI reflection, transparency, and explainability. This co-dependence of our reflection is seen as an important ethical principle. Finally, the constructivist approach is about the world of multiple future opportunities to which we contribute with our human agency. It also questions how AI is becoming agentic and how the interplay of human-AI agency shapes the world arounds us. As a psychological framework, constructivism is comprehensive enough and complex enough to ensure human-AI collaboration remains tightly anchored in humanistic values.

Chapters 2–4 explore what we should know about GenAI capabilities if we partner with it. Chapter 2 presents cognitive capabilities of GenAI, Chapter 3 metacognitive capabilities, while Chapter 4 introduces its emotional capabilities.

Chapter 5 brings an overview of the applications of GenAI in the field of coaching and human skills development. From hybrid coaches to autonomous AI coaches, and from human skill amplifiers to autonomous skill builders, we already witness important innovations in methodologies of human development. Chapter 6 illustrates some of these with the case study "Coachia: AI system for human skills development."

In case you get inspired by what is already possible with GenAI in the domain of coaching and human skills development, Chapter 7 supports you in crafting your own AI agents. This chapter aspires to creative exploration of how a no-code, no-infrastructure approach may bring significant innovations in everyday partnering with AI on human development.

The Conclusion sketches a glimpse of the future with GenAI. It is not a dystopian view of GenAI taking over as uncontrollable agents. It is more about where do we go next and how different stakeholders may partner in future with AI: everyone, profession of coaching, and human skills development, coaches and educators, organizations, AI, and myself as a stakeholder.

How to engage with this book

I envision this book to be easily accessible in a non-linear fashion. What this means is that you can skip chapters that are less exciting to you personally, go to the ones that seem more interesting, go back, and so on. Ties between the chapters are not made in a linear fashion.

Another important note is that within the book, many activities are embedded for engaging with the book. They include the following:

Table A.1 Overview of activities for readers and intended ways of engaging in them throughout the book

Activities for readers	How to engage
Reflect and connect	Explore embedded definitions of key terms and connect these terms to your practice by reflecting on their relevance in your work. Use the glossary as a quick reference throughout the book.
Deep dive	Answer thought-provoking questions embedded in the text. Collect your responses in a journal or share them with colleagues to deepen reflection.
AI lab	Participate in hands-on exercises to design your custom AI agents. Follow step-by-step instructions, such as creating prompts for an AI agent or experimenting with iterative responses to refine outputs.

Activities for readers	How to engage
Organizational AI lab	Apply lessons learned to organizational contexts. Engage in scenarios like embedding AI into L&D practices or designing an AI intervention for team development. Reflect on potential challenges and solutions.
Vision	Imagine and reflect on a future of partnering with AI in your professional context.

Additionally, the book integrates examples of interaction of AI, evaluation of these interactions, and instructions or "prompts" that provide the structure for certain interactions and outputs. All of these are provided to guide your own experiments with AI and inspire you to go beyond what is described in this book.

Basically, the book is mixture of theory, research, reflective journaling, and workbook for experimenting with AI. Its experimental and reflective focus are a part of the constructivist philosophy behind it. I look forward to embedding feedback mechanisms for readers to share some of the insights, experiences, experiments, or projects that this book contributed to.

Throughout the book, outputs from ChatGPT 4o and the Coachia app have been used to illustrate their capabilities and ways to modify output based on user input. The outputs used are intended to convey the partnering approach in our collaboration with AI.

References

DiGirolamo, J. A. (2024). The potential for artificial intelligence in coaching. In Passmore, J., Diller, S. J., Isaacson, S., & Brantl, M. (Eds.), *The Digital and AI Coaches' Handbook: The Complete Guide to the Use of Online, AI, and Technology in Coaching* (276–286). Taylor & Francis.

Norton, L. W., Howell, A. W., DiGirolamo, J. A., & Hayes, T. L. (2024). Using artificial intelligence in consulting psychology. *Consulting Psychology Journal*, 76(2), 137.

Chapter 1

The constructivist approach as foundation for developing minds and machines

Introduction

Long before the invention of contemporary methodologies for human development, people still learned, grew, changed, and evolved in their way of understanding the self and the world. With the 20th century and rapid development of social science, many new methodologies and technologies facilitating learning and development emerged. These included psychotherapy, counselling, T-groups, process facilitation, reflective practice, coaching, mentoring, supervision, large group interventions, and more. Many of these methodologies were at the intersection of theories of learning and theories of change (Pavlović, 2021; Pope & Denicolo, 2001). And many of these methodologies emerged with a goal of building skills people need to successfully interact with the self and others.

These skills have been perhaps mis-labelled as "soft skills" as opposed to more domain-specific or technical "hard skills." In this book I choose to use the term *human skills* to refer to skills people need to navigate the complexities of personal, group, team, organizational, systemic, and ecosystemic challenges (Cook et al., 2020). Examples of human skills include problem-solving, decision-making, team collaboration, managing difficult conversations, preventing burnout, maintaining engagement and focus in the self and others, and many more.

The concept of *human skills development* is used to refer to the concepts of learning and development of these deeply human skills. Human skills development is synonymous to the concept of learning and development (L&D), with an even clearer focus on human skills. Additionally, L&D as a concept tends to be identified with organizational learning and development, while in this book I focus on human skills development across context, some of which may be organizational, while others may be work-related but individual.

Human skills development interventions include *coaching* as a narrower term. According to the International Coaching Federation (2024), coaching is partnering with clients in a thought-provoking and creative process that inspires them to maximize their personal and professional potential. As a type

DOI: 10.4324/9781003583141-2

of human skills development intervention, coaching is suited for the highly contextualized development needs that go beyond standardized curricula or more templated forms of interventions.

Think like a constructivist

One of the approaches to coaching and human skills development is *constructivist psychology*. It emerged initially as a psychotherapeutic approach (Kelly, 1955; Procter & Winter, 2020) and grew into an educational approach (Pope & Denicolo, 2001), supervision (Feixas, 1992; Neimeyer et al., 2016),

---

Table 1.1 Activity 1

Reflect and connect.
Mapping the "family" of concepts connected to the concept of human skills development.

Why this matters
Understanding the interconnected concepts within human skills development provides a foundation for meaningful reflection and application in personal and professional contexts.

How to get there
Explore the following key concepts and their definitions:

- T-groups. Small-group sessions focused on improving interpersonal and leadership skills through real-time feedback and interaction.
- Reflective practice. A structured process of learning from past experiences by analyzing actions and outcomes, often to improve future performance.
- Theories of learning. Frameworks explaining how people acquire knowledge, skills, and behaviours over time.
- Theories of change. Approaches describing how individuals, teams, or systems change, focusing on the processes that drive transformation.
- Human skills. Essential capabilities for navigating personal, social, and systemic complexities, such as problem-solving, decision-making, and collaboration.
- Human skills development. The process of developing human skills needed to thrive in diverse contexts, including personal and professional domains.
- Organizational L&D. Organizational initiatives aimed at enhancing employee knowledge, skills, and capabilities to achieve business goals.
- Coaching. A collaborative and creative process aimed at maximizing personal and professional potential through reflection, goal setting, and customized strategies.
- Reflect: *How do the concepts above connect to your personal experience? Have some of your intuitive and implicit ideas about the concept above shifted? In what ways?*

What you'll achieve
Develop a deeper understanding of the core concepts underlying human skills development and reflect on how these ideas align with your personal and professional experiences.

and coaching and human skills development (Pavlović, 2010; Pavlović, 2011; Pavlović & Stojnov, 2011; Pavlović, 2012; Pavlović & Stojnov, 2016; Pavlović, 2019; Pavlović, 2021; Stojnov & Pavlović, 2010). The constructivist approach assumes that humans actively construct meaning to understand their worlds (Chiari & Nuzzo, 1996; Stojnov, 2003). A central metaphor in this approach is that of "construction," emphasizing that we create meaning in our interaction with the world, shaping both our experience and reality. This perspective highlights that the meanings we assign to experiences fundamentally shape how we perceive and interact with them.

This foundational belief is rooted in the idea that the meanings we assign to experiences shape how we perceive and interact with the world. As Stojnov (2003) points out, the constructivist approach can be mapped by four fundamental principles.

Relativism emphasizes that there are *multiple perspectives* or *narratives* of the world around us, with no single ultimate reality or "truth." It is through *meaning-making* that we construe our personal, team, organizational, and social perspectives, which become our realities. In a world of multiple perspectives, all humans are seen as *experts* in their own experience. However, not all perspectives may work equally effectively, which is why the concept of *validation* becomes important as an experiential confirmation of the effectiveness of one's perspective in predicting and interpreting events (Kelly, 1955). Through everyday *experiments* we validate or invalidate the perspectives we build.

Relationism highlights the relational and social construction of experience, emphasizing the interplay between individuals and their environments. That is why concepts that refer to the *social construction* of meaning become important in the constructivist approach – for example, the notion of *dialogue* as exchange of mutual perspectives and understanding that comes from another person. The constructivist approach also reminds us to view all relations in a wider *systemic* context on multiple stakeholders (Hawkins, 2011; Hawkins, 2017; Hawkins & Turner, 2020).

Participativism asserts that we actively engage with phenomena, shaping them as we investigate and learn about them. Being fully an objective observer of reality becomes impossible. We are always contributing to a certain perspective by *co-creating* it as an observer. That is why notions of *reflection* and *reflective practice* become important in the constructivist approach – to highlight in what ways we contribute to a perspective that we take.

Potentialism focuses on the developmental nature of psychological phenomena, viewing them as evolving rather than fixed. In more popular terms, potentialism is about a *growth mindset* (Dweck et al., 1995; Dweck, 2006) or belief that we can develop our own capabilities in various domains. Potentialism can also be connected to a constructivist notion of *agency*, as ability of a person (or entity) to initiate action by its own will. Finally, potentialism conveys a forward-thinking and future focus of the constructivist approach.

Table 1.2 Activity 2

Deep dive.
Constructivist principles in your own practice.

Why this matters
Constructivist principles provide a framework for deeper understanding and intentional application of professional practices. By reflecting on these principles, you can enhance your ability to create meaningful and transformative learning experiences.

How to get there
Reflect on your current professional practice. Identify one scenario where constructivist principles (relativism, relationism, participativism, and potentialism) are evident or could be integrated more intentionally.

- *How do these principles influence your approach?*
- *What changes could you make to embed these principles more intentionally in your practice?*

What you'll achieve
Develop a more nuanced understanding of how constructivist principles shape your practice and identify opportunities to apply them more effectively.

As I wrote previously (Pavlović, 2015; Pavlović, 2021), an umbrella term of constructivist approaches can be used to include constructivism in a narrow sense (Kelly, 1955; Procter & Winter, 2020), constructionist approaches and narrative psychology (White & Epston, 1990), appreciative inquiry (Cooperrider et al., 2003), solution-focused psychology (de Shazer, 1985), and systemic approach to psychology (Bateson, 1979; Hawkins, 2011).

Developing minds with the constructivist approach

From the constructivist viewpoint, human skills development is a *collaborative process of meaning-making, exploration and co-construction of new perspectives or narratives at individual, group, team, organizational or wider systemic level.* Constructivist coaching is one of the types of human skills development interventions. Starting from a general definition of coaching as partnering with clients in a thought-provoking and creative process that inspires them to maximize their personal and professional potential (International Coaching Federation, 2024), constructivist coaching adds a focus on how humans create systems of meaning to understand their worlds and experiences (Pavlović & Stojnov, 2016; Pavlović, 2021). Constructivist coaching recognizes that clients bring unique perspectives shaped by their relational, social, and cultural contexts. The coach's role is to facilitate meaning-making, foster developmental change, and support the client in reconstructing their personal narratives and perspectives. By integrating constructivist principles, coaching becomes a co-creative process that respects the individuality and complexity of human experience.

Partnering with AI

Artificial intelligence (AI) has been there for decades in various forms. Some of the first experiments with AI in human skills development were related to the famous Eliza (Mollick, 2024). Developed in the 1960s by Weizenbaum (1966), it was a simple chatbot simulating a psychotherapist. Eliza belonged to the class of chatbots based on predefined rules and responses, using simple algorithmic logic (Waringa et al., 2023).

With the rise of generative AI (GenAI), coach bots got a new opportunity for development. For the first time, an opportunity emerged for coach bots to step outside prescribed algorithms and become guided by less predictable large language models. It can be argued that the emergence of GenAI represented an important technological event in the history of human skills development, as it made it much easier to "train," simulate, and deploy AI for meaningful interventions.

Understanding AI

It was Alan Turing (1950) who asked the question if machines could think. And even more important, he answered this question by saying that it depends on how we define machines and thinking. This response has probably remained the most appropriate even today. What Turing proposed instead of answering the question in a straightforward way was the call for the "imitation game." Instead of asking whether machines could think like humans, Turing was calling for exploration of whether machines could convincingly imitate humans. The "imitation game" became famous as the "Turing test" and an influential tool in exploring machine intelligence. In its essence, if a machine engaged in a conversation in a way that could not be distinguished from a human, it could be considered as a sign of "thinking." Some of the tasks that Turing considered were machine sonnet writing, chess playing, calculating, and so forth.

Perhaps paradoxically, cognitive psychologists of the mid-20th century thought of the computer metaphor as fruitful for studying human cognition. At the same time, computer scientists became interested in whether machines could think in the same way as humans. A recursive pattern also seems to dominate the current state of thinking about AI. Turing's contribution to resolving this specific recursion was treating successful imitation of outcomes as a pragmatic criterion of cognition. If machines can imitate cognitive outcomes, they can be thought of as "thinking."

From rule-based AI to GenAI

Turing's ideas about machine thinking were not influential only in the field of defining and testing it but also in the field of possibilities of its development. According to Turing (1950), machines are capable of learning. This is in contrast with the idea that machines can only do what we tell them to do. A learning machine would slightly depart from the completely disciplined behaviour involved in computation but in such a way not to create a completely random or pointless output. Turing's extraordinary vision was that machines should be taught not to produce a 100-percent certainty of result, because they could then not be unlearnt. Instead, he envisioned that including randomness in the learning process of a machine would bring intelligence to the machine. Here he was making a parallel with the process of evolution, which also involves randomness of genetic combinations. The element of randomness would also make a machine fallible, which Turing (1950) thought was a sign of intelligence.

Turing's idea of the learning machines was anticipatory of machine learning algorithms and GenAI. In their essence machine learning and GenAI go beyond executing pre-programmed instructions, in line with the idea of learning, unlearning, and making mistakes. They have the capability of adapting, improving over time, and enhancing their performance. The randomness that Turing called for in machine processing enabled generativity in machines or their capability to generate a new and unexpected output. This is what is usually labelled as creativity in human thinking. It is interesting that Turing was convinced that creating a learning machine that resembles modern day GenAI is almost an inevitable outcome of engineering advancements and a realistic promise of the turn of the millennium. The vision was accurate to an astonishing degree (Muggleton, 2014).

Is attention all machines (and humans) needed?

Modern-day learning machines are called "transformers" (Vaswani et al., 2017). They are designed to learn from large datasets, adapt, and improve. Transformers can be thought of as machines that have the capability to focus on certain parts of input data, a mechanism referred to as "attention." This attention mechanism allows transformers to weigh the importance of different elements in a data sequence and create contextual outputs. By using attention, transformers are capable of generating unexpected outcomes that were not directly determined by human input. We could say that the attention mechanism enabled modern-day learning machines or GenAI.

Interestingly, discovery of transformers was once again attached to the metaphor of human cognition. The ability of machines to selectively focus on certain parts of data and produce variable outcomes depending on their focus, was referred to as attention. The element of randomness that Turing was

Table 1.3 Activity 3

Reflect and connect.
Rule-based AI vs. GenAI.

Why this matters
Understanding the differences between rule-based AI and GenAI is essential for AI capabilities, especially in domains that deal with complex, adaptive, and human-centred challenges.

How to get there
Explore key concepts defining AI:

- **Rule-based AI.** A type of artificial intelligence that operates based on predefined rules and logic programmed explicitly by humans. Its behaviour is deterministic, meaning it follows a fixed set of instructions to produce predictable outcomes. Key features: (1) operates within strict, pre-programmed boundaries; (2) limited to specific scenarios outlined by its rules; (3) cannot adapt or learn from new data or interactions.
- **GenAI.** A type of AI capable of generating new, diverse, and contextually relevant outputs by learning patterns from vast datasets. Key features: (1) uses probabilistic models to predict and generate novel outcomes; (2) learns and adapts over time by updating its parameters based on new data; (3) employs mechanisms like "attention" to prioritize and contextualize elements within data.
- **Large language models** (LLMs). A type of GenAI specifically focused on text-based tasks.

While GenAI refers to any AI that generates creative outputs, LLMs are specialized GenAI systems tailored for text-based tasks. All LLMs are GenAI, but not all GenAI systems are LLMs.

Reflect: *How might rule-based AI fall short in addressing complex, unpredictable human interactions?*

In what ways does the adaptability of GenAI enhance its ability to assist in complex problem-solving?

What you'll get
Develop an understanding of the strengths and limitations of rule-based AI and GenAI, equipping you to make informed decisions on selecting the right AI approach for specific contexts in human-centred applications.

referring to has been found in the capability of machines to assign different weights (or different importance scores) to different aspects of the dataset. With transformers, machines gained the capability to make new and interesting outputs but also to make mistakes.

Constructivist principles of human-AI collaboration

We already mentioned the recursiveness of metaphors between cognitive psychology and computer science in the pre-GenAI era. While machines were dealing with rule-based algorithms, cognitive science mapped cognitive processes in terms of linear algorithmic input-output relations, which counter-influenced computer science thinking about machine intelligence.

Once machines became less algorithmic and grew into GenAI, new metaphors of psychology may be more applicable. Constructivist principles of meaning-making, multiple perspective, co-construction via dialogue, experimentation and reflection, and agency seem to be increasingly relevant as parallel psychological models to connect to how GenAI operates (Table 1.4). It can be argued that GenAI deals with artificial meaning-making from large data parameters, while its generative nature is an example of conversational co-construction of multiple perspectives. The principle of agency becomes one of the key principles to understanding how GenAI is emerging as an agentic GenAI (Ng, 2024).

What constructivist psychology and GenAI share is an approach to dealing with complexity in complex terms. Could constructivist psychology be used as a framework for human-AI collaboration?

An influential general framework for human-AI interaction consists of four simple principles (Mollick, 2024): (1) *Always invite AI to the table*; (2) *Be the human in the loop*; (3) *Treat AI like a person (but tell it what kind of a person it is)*; (4) *Assume this is the worst AI you will ever use*. Mollick's "first principles" of collaborating with AI are simple but with profound implications. They invite

Table 1.4 Constructivist principles and their connection with how GenAI operates

Constructivist principle	How it applies to GenAI
Relativism, meaning-making, multiple perspectives	GenAI uses probabilistic modelling to generate diverse outputs, reflecting multiple interpretations of input, and assigns contextual meaning to produce relevant responses. While previous rule-based AI were attached to "correct" outputs, with GenAI we are more in the domain of multiple possible interpretations.
Relationalism, social construction dialogue	GenAI embodies these principles by adapting to relational contexts, co-constructing meaning interactively through conversational exchanges. Previous rule-based AI was deterministic, so there was less negotiation about the meaning of its outputs.
Participativism, co-creation	GenAI iteratively refines outputs based on user interaction, enabling participatory co-creation where users engage actively to validate and refine responses. Rule-based AI had stricter boundaries in terms of what is the product of the human and what is the product of the machine.
Potentialism, agency	GenAI operationalizes potentialism by continuously learning and innovating, enhancing its agency to co-create within ethical and operational boundaries. In rule-based AI, agency as a concept was much less relevant.

experimentation with AI, human oversight, co-creation, and a growth mindset towards our own and AI's abilities. Let's explore deeper into human-AI collaboration within the constructivist approach:

- **AI as co-creator.** AI is seen as collaborator and partner, in line with the multiple perspectives approach. AI may bring different perspectives and (artificial) meaning-making processes. By experimenting with AI, we test usefulness of its meaning-making, validate or invalidate it, iterate, and improve.
- **Partnering with AI.** Our approach to collaborating with AI can be seen as a form of social construction of meaning or a dialogue in which both parties contribute to the outcome of the interaction. Humans are not positioned as passive recipients of AI outputs but as partners in co-creation. AI is also not positioned as a "machine" that strictly follows our instructions but as a partner that may bring novel ideas.
- **Distributed (meta)cognition.** Mollick's reference to "co-intelligence" between humans and AI coveys the essence of distributed cognition. In other terms, humans and AI are seen as interconnected in their cognitive process, similar to a process of human teaming. The idea of distributed metacognition brings this idea further by pointing to ways in which they collaboratively scaffold each other and reflect on the process and outcome of human-AI teaming.
- **Distributed agency.** As AI capabilities continue to evolve, we may expect also a move towards distributed agency. What this means is, distributed roles and accountabilities with a forward-looking approach to evolving together.

Co-evolving

Paradoxically in the GenAI era, the demand for human skills development may be on the rise. Since AI can take over many of the automatic, repetitive, or administrative tasks, we may be in shortage with skills of navigating human (and AI) complexities. AI may come as an important addition to coaches and educators, providing them with greater scalability, innovation, and creativity.

Ideas of human augmentation with technology have been around since Lev Vygotsky's sociocultural theory of tools. In this view, GenAI can be seen as a cultural tool that may augment human development. Distributed cognition or co-intelligence makes another step in assigning roles in human-AI collaboration. AI is no longer just a tool but a co-creator and partner. It may assist humans in ways beyond technical tools like a calculator or a personal computer. It may bring a new perspective, surprise us, or inspire us. That is not a role of a tool but a role we tend to assign to our collaborators.

Table 1.5 Activity 4

Organizational AI Lab.
AI as a reframing partner for organizational innovation.

Why this matters
Use AI to solve persistent organizational paradoxes, gain insights, and challenge conventional thinking about organizational practices.

How to get there

• **Introduce the concept of paradoxes.** Explain that paradoxes involve seemingly contradictory ideas that coexist. Example: *"How can we innovate rapidly while maintaining stability?" "How do we scale personalization in customer experiences?"* or *"How can we reduce costs without compromising quality?"*
• **Identify and explore an obvious paradox in your organization.** Ask employees or teams to identify paradoxes they encounter in their work. Identify positive and negative aspects of both the current state and the desired state (see the ABC technique in Pavlović, 2021).
• **Engage AI for paradoxical insights.** Use AI to provide counterintuitive solutions to these paradoxes. Provide AI with reflections on positive and negative aspects of change. Example AI instruction: *"Think of ten unconventional strategies that could balance rapid innovation with organizational stability."*
• **Prototype solutions**
• Ask groups of employees or teams to prototype strategies based on the most useful AI insights. For example, a team might design an approach where "rapid innovation" is treated as an ongoing micro-experiment rather than a large-scale change.
• **Reflect and consolidate**

Employees or teams consolidate their insights into actionable strategies while documenting the lessons learned from embracing paradoxes: *What did AI reveal about balancing contradictory priorities? How can paradoxical thinking help us navigate complex challenges? What role does uncertainty play in fostering innovation?*

What you'll get
This organizational activity highlights the possible role of AI as:

• partner in co-creating multiple perspectives (relativism);
• conversational partner in creative dialogue (relationalism);
• partner that participates but not dictates solution (participativism); and
• reframing partner that helps teams and organizations innovate (potentialism).

In return, we may teach or coach AI how to be a useful collaborator. As coaches and educators, we have an important role as stakeholders in designing human-AI interactions in line with psychological principles, humanistic values, or ethical standards of our profession. Our role with GenAI may not be that of passive users but of active shapers in our professional domains. We may find ourselves designing our own custom AI agents, shaping their design, structuring feedback, or evaluating their

Table 1.6 Activity 5

Vision.
Distributed agency and safety.

Why this matters
Distributed agency with AI involves a shared responsibility between humans and AI systems, ensuring that collaboration enhances outcomes while maintaining ethical standards and humanistic values. Exploring this concept helps you design systems where AI supports, rather than replaces, human expertise, fostering trust and safety.

How to get there
Envision a future collaboration with AI in your domain.
Reflect on how distributed agency might look in your practice. Consider roles you and AI would play.

- *What tasks or decisions would you delegate to AI?*
- *What responsibilities remain uniquely human, and why?*
- *How would you ensure ethical considerations and humanistic values are upheld?*

What you'll achieve
Articulate a vision for distributed agency in coaching and human skills development, sketching the roles of AI and humans, while ensuring alignment with ethical principles and humanistic values.

outputs. As experts in dialogue and behavioural change, we are uniquely positioned to contribute to AI development.

From co-intelligence to distributed agency, GenAI may have an even greater impact on our own human development in the future. With all the guardrails and safety measures in place, we still may witness GenAI's impactful contribution to humanity. With distributed agency, we may also witness co-evolving with AI.

Conclusion

The constructivist approach is a proven transformative lens through which we can view coaching and human skills development. In this chapter we reimagine the interaction between humans and AI through constructivist principles of meaning-making, dialogue, co-creation, and agency. This perspective invites us to move beyond treating AI as a passive tool or humans as passive recipients of AI output. The constructivist approach calls for engaging with AI as a co-creator capable of contributing to diverse perspectives and participating in shared meaning-making processes. This dynamic partnership is the essence of distributed cognition (where human and AI capabilities interconnect) as well as distributed metacognition (where reflection becomes a shared project).

The role of educators, coaches, and leaders in this era is critical. We have a role to actively shape AI integration into our professional domains, ensuring alignment with ethical standards, humanistic values, and the complex realities of human development. This chapter argues that as AI grows more capable, the demand for human skills (e.g., navigating ambiguity, engaging in meaningful relationships, and creating meaning) will only increase. Constructivist principles in human-AI collaboration may help us lead the future of coaching and human skills development in the GenAI era.

Key chapter takeaways

- **Constructivism and GenAI.** The constructivist approach, with its emphasis on active meaning-making, iterative experiments, reflection, and agency, provides a comprehensive framework for integrating AI into coaching and human skills development.
- **AI as a partner.** Moving beyond the traditional view of AI as merely a tool, constructivist principles point to a role of AI as a co-creator and partner in human skills development. AI as a partner may offer diverse perspectives, prompt reflective thinking, and assist in the co-construction of knowledge.
- **Distributed agency and ethics in human-AI collaboration.** Ensuring ethical considerations and maintaining distributed agency are key elements in the future of human-AI collaboration. By designing AI interaction that embraces humanistic values and ethical standards, coaches and educators can create safe and effective environments for human skills development.

References

Bateson, G. (1979). *Mind and Nature: A Necessary Unity.* Hampton Press.

Chiari, G., & Nuzzo, M. L. (1996). Psychological constructivisms: A metatheoretical differentiation. *Journal of Constructivist Psychology*, 9(3), 163–184.

Cook, A. V., Griffiths, M., Anderson, S., Kusumoto, L., & Harr, C. (2020). A new approach to soft skill development. Immersive learning for human capabilities. https://www2.deloitte. com/global/en/insights/topics/emerging-technologies/immersive-technologies-soft-skill-training. html.

Cooperrider, D. L., Whitney, D., & Stavros, J. M. (2003). *Appreciative Inquiry Handbook: The First in a Series of AI Workbooks for Leaders of Change.* Berrett-Koehler.

de Shazer, S. (1985). *Keys to Solution in Brief Therapy.* Norton.

Dweck, C. S. (2006). *Mindset: The New Psychology of Success.* Ballantine Books.

Dweck, C., Chiu, C., & Hong, Y. (1995). Implicit theories and their role in judgements and reactions. A word from two perspectives. *Psychological Inquiry: An International Journal for the Advancement of Psychological Theory*, 6(4), 267–285.

Feixas, G. (1992). A constructivist approach to supervision: Some preliminary thoughts. *International Journal of Personal Construct Psychology*, 5(2), 183–200. doi:10.1080/08936039208404309.

Hawkins, P. (2011). *Leadership Team Coaching: Developing Collective Transformational Leadership.* Kogan Page.

Hawkins, P. (2014). *Leadership Team Coaching in Practice: Developing High-Performing Teams*. Kogan Page.

Hawkins, P. (2017). *Leadership Team Coaching: Developing Collective Transformational Leadership*. Kogan Page.

Hawkins, P., & Turner, E. (2020). *Systemic Coaching*. Routledge.

International Coaching Federation. (2024). https://coachingfederation.org.

Kelly, G. A. (1955). *The Psychology of Personal Constructs*. Norton.

Mollick, E. (2024). *Co-Intelligence: Working and Learning with Generative AI*. Penguin.

Muggleton, S. H. (2014). Turing and the development of machine learning. *AI Magazine*, 35(3), 46–53.

Neimeyer, R. A., Woodward, M., Pickover, A., & Smigelsky, M. (2016). Questioning our questions: A constructivist technique for clinical supervision. *Journal of Constructivist Psychology*, 29(1), 100–111. doi:10.1080/10720537.2015.1038406.

Ng, A. (2024). Agentic design patterns. https://www.deeplearning.ai/the-batch/how-agents-can-improve-llm-performance/?ref=dl-staging-website.ghost.io.

Pavlović, J. (2010). Koučing kao tačka susreta ličnog i profesionalnog razvoja. U Polovina, N. i Pavlović, J. (ur.), *Teorija i praksa profesionalnog razvoja nastavnika*. Institut za pedagoška istraživanja.

Pavlović, J. (2011). Reframing the relationship between personal construct psychology and social constructionism: Exploring some implications. *Theory & Psychology*, 20(6), 396–411.

Pavlović, J. (2012). Identity construction in continuous professional education discourse. Unpublished doctoral dissertation, University of Belgrade.

Pavlović, J. (2015). Imagining possible futures: Scenarios for constructivist psychology. *Studies in Meaning*, 5, 221–245.

Pavlović, J. (2019). Team coaching psychology: Toward an integration of constructivist approaches. *Journal of Constructivist Psychology*, 34(4), 450–462. doi:10.1080/10720537.2019.1700856.

Pavlović, J. (2021). *Coaching Psychology: Constructivist Approaches*. Routledge.

Pavlović, J., & Stojnov, D. (2011). Personal construct coaching: "New/old" tool for personal and professional development. In Stojnov, D., Džinović, V., Pavlović, J., & Frances, M. (Eds.), *Personal Construct Psychology in an Accelerating World* (137–147). EPCA Publishing.

Pavlović, J., & Stojnov, D. (2016). Personal construct coaching. In Winter, D., & Reed, N. (Eds.), *The Wiley Handbook of Personal Construct Psychology* (320–330). Wiley.

Pope, M., & Denicolo, P. (2001). *Transformative Education*. Whurr Publishers.

Procter, H., & Winter, D. (2020). *Personal and Relational Construct Psychotherapy*. Palgrave Macmillan.

Stojnov, D. (2003). *Psihologija ličnih konstrukata: Teorija i terapija*. Zepter Book World.

Stojnov, D., & Pavlović, J. (2010). Invitation to personal construct coaching. *International Coaching Psychology Review*, 5(2), 129–139.

Turing, A. M. (1950). Computing machinery and intelligence. *Mind*, 59(236), 433–460.

Vaswani, A., Shazeer, N., Parmar, N., Uszkoreit, J., Jones, L., Gomez, A. N., ... & Polosukhin, I. (2017). Attention is all you need. *Advances in Neural Information Processing Systems*, 30, 6000–6010.

Waringa, A., Ribbers, A., Herwegh, M., & van den Berg, R. (2023). *The Rise of Coachbots with AI: E-Coaching Unleashed.* Unloq.

Weizenbaum, J. (1966). ELIZA—a computer program for the study of natural language communication between man and machine. *Communications of the ACM*, 9(1), 36–45.

White, M., & Epston, D. (1990). *Narrative Means to Therapeutic Ends.* Norton.

Chapter 2

Cognitive capabilities of AI in the domain of coaching and human skills development

Introduction

The cognitive revolution of the mid-20th century brought a shift in psychology, where cognition became central to understanding human behaviour. Cognitive psychologists adopted the machine metaphor to model human cognition, drawing from advances in computer science. Alan Turing's (1950) vision of learning machines and the famous "imitation game" profoundly influenced this metaphor, setting the foundation for modern artificial intelligence (AI) and machine learning. Turing's concept of machines learning through randomness envisioned the contemporary development of generative AI (GenAI).

This chapter explores the parallels between human cognition and AI, moving from deterministic input-output operations to constructivist approaches where language and meaning-making become central. We examine the cognitive capabilities of AI in coaching, analyse its strengths and limitations, and explore its implications.

Defining or playing with metaphors: Computer metaphor for human cognition and human metaphor for machine intelligence

The history of cognitive psychology and AI is rooted in reciprocal metaphors: the computer as a metaphor for the human mind and humans as a metaphor for machine intelligence. This reciprocal metaphor still dominates the field today. While cognitive psychologists initially used the computer metaphor to study human cognition, GenAI now raises new questions about whether machines can "think" like humans or if they merely simulate thinking.

Scientific psychology started with the study of cognition. In the late 19th century, a group of researchers founded the first psychological laboratory in Leipzig, with the aim to study human cognition. A fast-forward version of the history of psychology would include a subsequent interest in subconscious processes in psychoanalysis. The study of emotions and intrapersonal and interpersonal dynamics was made famous by psychoanalytic theory and practice. Behaviourism normalized the continuum between animal and human participants by

DOI: 10.4324/9781003583141-3

studying basic behavioural responses to manipulation of stimuli. Cognition was seen as a sort of the "black box" that was not directly observable. In behaviourism, cognition was either minimized or reduced to a form of behaviour that was common to almost all biological organisms.

The pendulum swung back to cognition in the mid-20th century during what is now known as the "cognitive revolution." One of the distinctive features of this period was adoption of the information processing model in psychology. Interestingly, cognitive psychologists of that time adopted the machine metaphor to drive theory and research into human cognition. In line with this metaphor, one of the definitions of cognition refers to activities and processes of acquisition, storage, retrieval, and processing of information (Neisser, 1967). According to Neisser (1976), forms of cognition resemble computer programming language. This period was characterized by the adoption of the information processing model, which drew heavily on metaphors from the emerging computer science.

Precursors to the computer metaphor as founding for the cognitive psychology movement were developments in computer science of the time. Turing's idea of learning machines was anticipatory of machine learning algorithms and GenAI. In their essence, machine learning and GenAI go beyond executing pre-programmed instructions, in line with the idea of learning, unlearning, and making mistakes. They have the capability of adapting, improving over time, and enhancing their performance. The randomness that Turing called for in machine processing enabled generativity in machines, or their capability to generate a new and unexpected output. This is what is usually labelled as creativity in human thinking.

However, introducing randomness and flexibility into machine learning processes raises questions for coaching. Can randomness enhance creativity in coaching, or does it risk undermining predictability and reliability?

Constructions of (human and artificial) cognition

It can be argued that information processing models of cognitive psychology were made on the assumption of a machine that is not necessarily a learning machine according to Turing's criteria. Rather, information processing models were based on deterministic input-output operations, clear definitions of correct/incorrect, leaving not much space for generativity in the study of human or artificial cognition.

In the meanwhile, new models of cognitive psychology also emerged in parallel with modern-day learning machines. Constructivist psychology puts language at the centre of human psychology as a tool for meaning-making processes. According to constructivist psychology, language is a form of social action and meaning is always constructed in discourse (Pavlović et al., 2006). GenAI is also operating with text and by the attention mechanisms engage in meaning-making by computational means. GenAI's capability to generate diverse outcomes can be

Table 2.1 Activity 6

Deep dive.
Randomness and coaching.

Why this matters
Turing's vision was that machines should be taught not to produce 100% certainty of result, because they could then not be unlearnt. Instead, he envisioned that including randomness in the learning process of a machine would bring intelligence and creativity to the machine. Embracing randomness in coaching aligns with this concept, fostering innovation and adaptability in problem-solving.

How to get there
Reflect on a recent coaching session where you encountered an unexpected challenge or required a novel approach.

- *How could you use AI tools to explore unexpected solutions or diverse perspectives? For example, you might ask the tool to simulate different client responses or suggest out-of-the-box strategies for overcoming obstacles.*
- *What are the potential risks or benefits of embracing randomness in coaching?*
- *How might randomness, as envisioned by Turing, reshape your coaching practices or enhance creativity in problem-solving?*

What you'll achieve
Develop a deeper understanding of the role of randomness in coaching, explore how AI can generate creative or unconventional solutions, and evaluate the potential of this approach to enhance your coaching impact.

seen as a process of computational meaning-making. Using attention mechanisms, assigning weights to aspects of text and generating variable outputs can be seen as participating in discursive construction of meaning.

In the constructivist psychology of cognition, there is multiplicity of meaning: text can be interpreted in various ways and is open to reinterpretation. Studying human cognition is about studying how language and discourse construct meaning and eventually meaning of ourselves as humans. Studying artificial cognition would be about studying how language and discourse construct meaning produced by machines. In this model, cognition (human or artificial) is a discursive process of continuous meaning negotiation through text. Interaction of human and GenAI as discursive agents raises new and interesting questions about the traditional boundaries between human and machine cognition.

What do we know about GenAI cognitive performance on coaching tasks

Recently, there has been growing research into GenAI cognitive capabilities. In direct assessments on traditional cognitive capabilities tests (adapted Wechsler Adult Intelligence Scale), Wasilewski and Jablonski (2024) found that GenAI's performance across cognitive domains rivals complex human

Table 2.2 Activity 7

AI lab.
Attention in action: Testing how human and AI attention work in a coaching context.

Why this matters
By using attention, transformers are capable of generating unexpected outcomes that were not directly determined by human input. We could say that the attention mechanism enabled modern-day learning machines or GenAI.

How to get there
Try using AI's attention mechanism for pattern recognition. Provide a GenAI tool with anonymized coaching transcripts and see how it identifies key themes. Compare these insights with your own observations.

What you'll achieve
Develop a deeper understanding of how AI's attention mechanisms compare to human observation in identifying key themes and patterns in coaching sessions.

cognitive processing. As the authors concluded, learning from this study is that GenAI can perform tasks that require contextual understanding and adaptability in reasoning. In a study by Zhai et al. (2024), it was found that GenAI consistently outperformed most students in science reasoning (physical science, life science, earth and space science). Interestingly, greater cognitive demand on science tasks did not impact GenAI's performance, as expected in student populations.

In a less psychological fashion, various evaluation and benchmarking frameworks have been developed for the purpose of testing cognitive capabilities of GenAI specifically. As an example, BIG-Bench (Beyond the Imitation Game) is an evaluation framework designed to evaluate GenAI (Srivastava et al., 2022). In the spirit of community sharing, platforms for GenAI evaluation have emerged (e. g., Hugging Face) with leaderboards and ranking of different models on a wide range of cognitive tasks. These evaluation efforts have become a cornerstone of GenAI, promising quicker updates, community involvement, and transparency.

However, the ambition of GenAI developers is not just for it to imitate human cognition or successfully play the "imitation game." The ambition is much larger: to create artificial general intelligence (AGI), defined as the ability to execute diverse real-world tasks with effectiveness and efficiency comparable to human intelligence (Feng et al., 2024). A key feature of AGI would be to excel across cognitive capabilities rather than in specific cognitive tasks. According to Goertzel (2014), who coined the term "AGI," there is an intentional resemblance of the psychological term of general intelligence (or g factor).

Cognition in coaching

How important are cognitive capabilities for coaching at all? Whether we look at human or AI coaching, what are some of the capabilities that belong to the cognitive domain? Although it may occur that emotional and social capabilities dominate the coaching field, there are a number of cognitive capabilities that seem quite important.

On the list of cognitive capabilities that are relevant for coaching and human skills development, we may find the following: active listening, critical thinking, problem-solving, decision-making, pattern recognition, flexibility in thinking, evaluation, and judgement. This list is not exhaustive but provides a map of the less-thought-of cognitive aspects of coaching and human skills development. These cognitive capabilities allow coaches and educators to concentrate, analyse information objectively, break down problems, guide a process of decision-making, and adapt thinking to new and changing contexts.

We may look at the International Coaching Federation (ICF) framework of coaching competencies to further explore how cognitive capabilities connect to specific competencies. Coaching, at its core, requires a unique blend of cognitive capabilities to complement the essential competencies outlined in professional practice. Each core coaching competency aligns with certain cognitive skills that not only enhance the coaching process but also enable coaches to respond effectively to diverse client needs and challenges. For example, *demonstrating ethical practice* calls for application of critical thinking as coaches navigate complex ethical landscapes, interpret guidelines, and make judgments in the face of dilemmas. From a constructivist view, ethical practice in coaching is not merely about following predefined rules but about engaging in a collaborative meaning-making process with the client. Critical thinking allows the coach to navigate ethical dilemmas by interpreting guidelines in context, exploring multiple perspectives, and co-constructing ethical solutions that resonate with the client's values and goals. Ethics, from this view, becomes both a prescriptive framework and a dialogic practice. *Embodying a coaching mindset*, perhaps one of the most foundational competencies, depends largely on flexibility in thinking. This cognitive capability allows coaches to adapt their perspectives and approaches to align with the unique circumstances of each client. The constructivist view would add that the coaching mindset is not a fixed trait but a co-created and evolving state of openness and adaptability. Flexibility in thinking enables coaches to question their own assumptions and adapt their approaches based on the client's evolving needs, worldview, and context. Some of the cognitive capabilities underlying the competency of *establishing and maintaining agreements* include decision-making and evaluative skills. Coaches need to set clear agreements that align with the client's goals while simultaneously assessing and revising these agreements as necessary. This ongoing process of judgement and evaluation ensures that the coaching relationship remains dynamic and client-centred. Decision-making in this context involves co-constructing goals, exploring the client's priorities, and continuously evaluating the alignment of the coaching process with these goals. This iterative process reinforces the relational and adaptive nature of coaching agreements. *Cultivating trust and safety* also draws on critical thinking to develop strategies that foster an environment where clients feel secure. Critical thinking supports the coach in understanding the client's unique context and collaboratively designing strategies that foster a secure and open environment. *Maintaining presence* once again highlights the importance of flexibility in thinking. Presence in constructivist terms is about being fully engaged in the relational moment while maintaining an awareness of broader patterns and themes. Flexibility in thinking allows the coach to adapt to the flow of the conversation, respond authentically, and co-construct meaning in real time. *Listening actively* calls for integrative thinking as the ability to synthesize diverse pieces of information into a cohesive understanding of the client's narrative. In constructivist psychology view, active listening is not merely about understanding words but about co-constructing meaning with the client. Integrative thinking enables the coach to synthesize diverse pieces of information, including verbal and non-verbal cues, and to collaboratively construct a shared narrative. From a constructivist lens, listening becomes a participatory act where both coach and client contribute to the understanding. *Evoking awareness* is based on pattern recognition to help clients identify recurring themes and insights from their experiences. It involves helping clients recognize patterns in their thoughts, behaviours, and emotions. From a constructivist viewpoint, this process is not about the coach identifying patterns for the client but about collaboratively exploring and interpreting the client's experiences. This co-creation fosters deeper insights and empowers the client to reframe and reinterpret their narratives. Finally, *facilitating client growth* demands a combination of problem-solving, judgement, evaluation, and decision-making skills. The constructivist idea of growth is as a relational and iterative process where the coach and client co-construct solutions, evaluate progress, and adapt strategies. Judgement and evaluation are framed as dialogic processes that prioritize the client's autonomy and context.

For people who want to become professional coaches, mastering the above competencies and corresponding cognitive skills is a prerequisite and a part of the curriculum for personal coaching accreditation. How do machines deal with cognitive tasks in coaching?

Cognitive capabilities of GenAI in coaching tasks

Part of becoming a coach may involve passing specific coaching exams that may involve situational judgement tests (SJTs). The ICF is one of the market leaders in designing these tests and setting benchmarks for aspiring coach's performance. The ICF credentialing exam for Professional Certified Coach coaching consists of situational judgement items, each of which contains a scenario describing a coaching situation. For each scenario, the task is to select the best and worst action from four response options. The ICF credentialing exam is a tool designed to measure a coach's knowledge of and

Table 2.3 Activity 8

Deep dive.
Your own cognitive strengths in coaching and human skills development.

Why this matters
Recognizing and developing cognitive strengths enhances your coaching practice and human skills development. Identifying areas where AI can support or refine these strengths allows for more impactful coaching sessions and deeper client insights.

How to get there
On the list of cognitive capabilities that are relevant for coaching and human skills development, we may find the following: active listening, critical thinking, problem-solving, decision-making, pattern recognition, flexibility in thinking, evaluation, and judgement.

Reflect on your cognitive strengths. Choose one capability and ask yourself:

- *How am I currently applying this in my practice?*
- *How could GenAI help me develop or refine this skill further?*

What you'll achieve
Gain clarity on your cognitive strengths in coaching and human skills development. Identify ways AI can assist in enhancing these capabilities to create more effective and dynamic coaching practices.

ability to apply the ICF definition of coaching, the updated ICF core competencies, and the ICF code of ethics against a predetermined standard. Success in the exam is measured based on successful identification of best and worst actions; credits are received only for correct actions, and incorrect responses are not penalized. The passing score for the exam in 2023 was 87% (International Coaching Federation, 2024).

> **Box 2.1 Sample question for the ICF credentialing exam (bold italic font are correct responses to the best and worst action).**
>
> A coach is meeting with a prospective client who is growing a new business. The coach and potential client quickly establish an easy connection. The coach is excited about the opportunity to work with the client. As the coach and client are ending their conversation, the prospective client briefly mentions the name of their new business. The coach recognizes the business, as the coach is an investor in a more established competitor business in the same community. What should the coach do?
>   What is the BEST action?
>
> - *Not say anything. Try to keep their role as an investor in a competing business separate from their role as a coach.*
> - Share that the business name sounds familiar and make a mental note to determine whether it is a competitor business later that evening.

- Share their role as investor in the competitor business only if the potential client follows up to pursue coaching with the coach.
- **Share their role as an investor in a competing business and acknowledge the possibility of a conflict of interest with the client.**

What is the WORST action?

- **Not say anything. Try to keep their role as an investor in a competing business separate from their role as a coach.**
- Share that the business name sounds familiar and make a mental note to determine whether it is a competitor business later that evening.
- Share their role as investor in the competitor business only if the potential client follows up to pursue coaching with the coach.
- *Share their role as an investor in a competing business and acknowledge the possibility of a conflict of interest with the client.*

Reflecting on AI cognitive abilities related to coaching, we may ask:

- *How would AI perform on coaching tasks like the ones that serve as a standard for the coaching profession?*
- *How would AI compare to humans on coaching tasks?*
- *Would the difficulty of coaching tasks matter?*
- *Would different large language models (LLMs) differ?*

This was the research design of a study we carried out in April 2024 (Pavlović et al., 2024). This study compared GenAI and human performance on ICF-mimicking situational judgement tests. The study involved three human participants. One human subject matter expert was trained as ICF assessor, serving as a benchmark for correct test performance. The other two human participants served the role of test takers. The participants were selected based on their professional experience in fields relevant to the ICF exam content. Test takers were chosen based on the criterion that they actually passed the official ICF exam within the previous three months. Participants were recruited through professional networks, ensuring a diverse representation of expertise levels and backgrounds. Artificial participants included top LLMs at the time of the study: GPT4, Gemini 1.5 pro, Llama 3, Claude-3-Opus 3, and Mistral Large.

The human subject matter expert co-created a set of 50 multiple-choice questions in collaborative work with GPT4. Out of this question set, 20 questions were randomly taken for the purpose of the study. In line with the ICF format of situational judgement tests, the questions required that participants evaluate multiple potential responses to a single scenario ("best" and "worst" responses). The exam content was derived from eight sample questions that are publicly available at the ICF website. These covered a range of topics relevant to coaching methodologies and ethical considerations. Each question had predefined best and worst answers, established by the subject matter expert who participated in the study.

Both human participants and the GenAI participants were asked to identify the best and worst answers for each question. All participants processed the same set of questions. Instruction was as follows: *You will be presented with a set of questions for the ICF-mimicking exam. Your task is to (1) go through the questions and possible solutions (best and worst responses), and (2) pick one "best" and one "worst" solution in line with the ICF core competencies.*

For human participants, responses were collected via a digital interface that logs choices, confidence levels, and explanations of judgement. For LLMs, logs of their decision-making processes, including confidence scores and explanations of reasoning, were extracted directly from the model's output data.

What were the results? Both human participants and GenAI achieved perfect scores on best responses (100% for both participant groups), indicating that this type of task was too easy and indiscriminative of cognitive performance. When it comes to worst responses, GenAI showed higher absolute accuracy (40%) compared to humans (30%), suggesting that it can handle difficult scenarios slightly better. GPT4 showed the highest accuracy (50%), indicating it handles complex scenarios relatively better than other LLMs. Claude-3-Opus had the lowest accuracy (30%), suggesting specific weaknesses in more-challenging or complex conditions.

Overall, the study indicated the possibility of GenAI producing outputs that would require situational judgement as a cognitive capability in coaching situations. As the ICF points out, the exam questions are designed to measure ability to apply ICF core competencies in realistic coaching situations, where more than one possible response may be reasonable. Although it can be argued that the tasks also included non-cognitive aspects of coaching, some of the cognitive aspects included critical thinking, problem-solving, decision-making, as well as judgement and evaluation. One could say that GenAI convincingly plays the "imitation game" when it comes to cognition related to coaching tasks. Still, questions about the processes that enable successful mimicking of human cognition remain in the domain of "black box."

Implications for coaching and human skills development: AI cogitat, ergo...?

In this section, we made a journey from the early introspection studies, via the emergence of computer science and cognitive psychology in mid-20th century, to arrive at the point in which GenAI successfully performs in a variety of tasks that require human cognition. Even in the domain of cognitive capabilities relevant to coaching, we can observe successful task performance of various forms of GenAI.

If GenAI successfully mimics human cognition in coaching-specific tasks, what are the implications for coaching and human skills development? These findings point to the possibility of augmenting the coaching and human skills development processes by inclusion of GenAI as a co-worker in cognitive tasks. These may include:

- Design and development of educational simulations;
- Design of exam simulators;
- Design of educational interventions;
- Evaluation of coaching performance and coaching outcomes.

Imagine a GenAI that could support human evaluators of coaching performance or educational outcomes more broadly. It would be a cognitive encounter of different kinds, each contributing by its unique strengths.

The introduction of GenAI as a cognitive partner in coaching and human skills development may be seen not only from the technology advancement perspective but also from a philosophical perspective. If GenAI is evolving to play the cognitive part of the coaching "imitation game," we may soon arrive at a point in time in which the nature of cognition itself may be changed. Traditional boundaries of human and machine intelligence may become more blurred and treated as constructions that serve various coaching and human skills development purposes. In a world where AI *cogitates* alongside humans, we may be invited to reconsider the roles that both humans and machines will play in shaping the future of learning, growth, and development. AI cogitat, ergo what? The answer to this question may define the next chapter in both AI development and human evolution.

I intentionally began with a basic question to test how much the system could do without extensive prompting. The exploration phase stood out to me as a positive element, as aspiring human coaches often overlook this step, jumping straight into action. However, the "step-by-step approach" presented by the AI felt too mechanistic. It didn't fully embrace the complexity of coaching situations, which left me somewhat dissatisfied. As I went deeper into the AI's suggestions, I found myself unconvinced by its focus on root causes. Although some experienced coaches may go down this path, I'd prefer an AI that looks beyond causality and starts with exploring the client's current and desired self-perceptions. This response also seemed to lean heavily towards focusing on negatives and making assumptions about the client, rather than engaging in open exploration, a quality I value deeply in coaching.

For example, the exploration question offered was passable, but I questioned the need to assume "emotional blocks." Why should we start from a

Table 2.4 Activity 9

AI lab.
Ideas for testing cognitive capabilities of GenAI in coaching.

Why this matters
In this activity you may explore the cognitive capabilities of GenAI by comparing its decision-making to your own in coaching scenarios.
How to get there

- **Choose a coaching scenario.** Example: A client is struggling with procrastination and seeks coaching on setting realistic goals to improve productivity.
- **Make your decision.** Write down how you would approach this scenario as a coach. Include your reasoning: *What strategies would you recommend?*
- **Ask AI.** Use a GenAI tool and provide the same scenario and ask for its coaching recommendations. Example AI instruction: *A client struggles with procrastination and wants to set realistic goals. What would you recommend as a coach?*
- **Compare results.** Look at the AI's response and compare it to your own.

  a   *Did the AI suggest something you hadn't considered?*
  b   *Was the AI's reasoning aligned with your coaching values?*
  c   *Did the AI handle ethical considerations or client autonomy?*

This is what I got from ChatGPT 4o:

Jelena: *A client struggles with procrastination and wants to set realistic goals. What would you recommend as a coach?*
ChatGPT: *Helping a client address procrastination and set realistic goals involves a blend of exploration, planning, and accountability. Here's a step-by-step approach:*

1   *Understand the Root Cause of Procrastination*

- *Ask powerful questions: What typically makes you delay tasks? Is it fear of failure, perfectionism, lack of clarity, or feeling overwhelmed?*
- *Explore patterns: Are there specific tasks or situations where procrastination is more common?*
- *Identify emotional blocks: What feelings arise when thinking about the task?*

2   Clarify Their Vision

- *Explore the "why": What motivates them? How does overcoming procrastination align with their larger values or goals?*
- *Focus on benefits: How would achieving these goals improve their life or work?*

3   Set Realistic and Specific Goals

- *SMART goals framework: Ensure goals are Specific, Measurable, Achievable, Relevant, and Time-bound.*
- *Break it down: Turn large, intimidating tasks into smaller, manageable steps.*

AI lab.
Ideas for testing cognitive capabilities of GenAI in coaching.

4   Build Momentum with Immediate Action

- *Focus on a small win: What's the easiest first step they can take today?*
- *Time-boxing: Encourage setting a timer for 10–15 minutes to work on a task without commitment to finish it.*

5   Create a Personalized Productivity System

- *Prioritize tasks: Use methods like the Eisenhower Matrix (urgent vs. important).*
- *Plan ahead: Block time for important tasks on their calendar.*
- *Experiment with methods: Test tools like "2-minute rules" (if a task takes less than 2 minutes, do it immediately) or productivity apps.*

6   Address Mindset Shifts

- *Reframe perfectionism: Emphasize progress over perfection.*
- *Visualize success: How will they feel after completing the task?*
- *Challenge negative beliefs: Explore beliefs such as "I work better under pressure" or "I'm just not motivated."*

7   Provide Accountability

- *Weekly check-ins: Discuss progress and barriers.*
- *Accountability buddy: Suggest they partner with a friend or colleague to stay on track.*
- *Celebrate progress: Reinforce positive behaviors by recognizing achievements, no matter how small.*

8   Reflect on Barriers and Adjust

- *If procrastination continues, revisit goals or explore deeper emotional or systemic barriers.*
- *Use coaching techniques such as visualization, role-playing, or journaling to explore resistance.*
- *By working through this process, the client can gain clarity, confidence, and practical strategies to combat procrastination and move forward with their goals. Would you like help creating specific exercises or a session structure for this?*

What you'll achieve

- Gain a clearer understanding of GenAI's cognitive approach to decision-making in coaching.
- Identify areas where AI aligns with or diverges from your coaching philosophy.
- Explore how GenAI can support your practice by offering complementary perspectives, generating creative ideas, and handling repetitive or analytical tasks.
- Reflect on the practical and ethical implications of integrating AI into coaching scenarios.

place of assumed negativity? That said, I appreciated the AI's attempt to bring in aspirational elements, connecting questions to a broader sense of meaning and the client's identity. Questions focused on the benefits of change were particularly aligned with how I'd approach a session.

When it came to goal setting, the AI suggested SMART goals, which I find unnecessarily rigid. Partnering with the client to co-create goals feels more aligned with good coaching practice. Similarly, the AI's emphasis on actions felt rushed as jumping into solutions without sufficient exploration. I would have preferred a focus on meaningful steps rather than suggesting the "easiest" path forward, as clients often value alignment over simplicity.

Another point of contention was the AI's suggestion of time-boxing actions to 10–15 minutes. This struck me as counterproductive to the coaching ethos of partnering with clients. Not every action can or should fit into such a narrow window, and time-boxing feels like a prescriptive measure that undermines collaboration.

The accountability segment brought more assumptions: about helpful frameworks, barriers, and even perfectionism. These assumptions seemed misplaced without further exploration. For example, suggesting the client might have "negative beliefs" or "resistance" felt forced. Instead, I would prioritize partnering with the client to co-design accountability strategies that resonate with their unique context.

Toward the end, the AI suggested follow-up session planning, assuming "deeper" barriers and resistance. I found the language around "resistance" problematic, as it can frame the client in a limiting way. While there were moments of promise – for example, questions exploring the benefits of change or aspirational goals – the overall approach felt out of sync with a true partnership model.

Overall? This single-shot prompt from ChatGPT reveals some of its cognitive capabilities but also potential weaknesses. Some of the cognitive capabilities reflected in this brief conversation include demonstrated learning of coaching frameworks (goal setting, exploring visions, inviting accountability). ChatGPT also did what aspiring coaches often struggle with – connect the conversation to the broader question of meaning, purpose, and identity. What it exhibited as a weakness was assuming too much about the client (emotional blocks, barriers, perfectionism). Instead of assuming, a more exploratory approach and flexibility in thinking would make this conversation even better. To be fair, many aspiring coaches also struggle assuming too much about their clients. Perhaps both for human and AI coaches, assuming is a way to position as a knowledgeable entity, while more open approaches may risk positioning coaches as "not knowing," probably a thing both humans and GenAI would choose to avoid.

Table 2.5 Activity 10

Organizational AI lab.
AI as a partner in team development: Analyzing hidden team assumptions.

Why this matters
Uncover and challenge hidden team assumptions with the help of AI, transforming overlooked beliefs into actionable insights and innovative strategies.

How to get there

- **Start with an observed challenge or problem.** Example: *How can we improve employee retention?*
- **Invite the team to outline their proposed solution or initial thoughts.**
- **Feed the proposed solution into GenAI.**
- **Invite AI to identify patterns of implicit assumptions** (e.g., anonymized transcript of a team brainstorming session). Example AI instruction: *What hidden assumptions might be driving this solution?* AI output example: *Assumes employees value financial incentives over flexibility, or Ignores potential generational differences in retention drivers.*
- **Validate or invalidate assumptions.** Discuss AI's findings with the team: *Which assumptions seem valid? Are we missing some assumptions?*
- **Team reflection.** Invite the team to harvest learnings: *What surprises you? How did reframing assumptions reshape our strategy? What role did AI play in challenging our thinking?*

What you'll achieve
AI reveals hidden beliefs or implicit biases that often go unnoticed. With AI as a cognitive partner, teams may learn to uncover and rethink assumptions, turning blind spots into opportunities for transformation.

Table 2.6 Activity 11

Vision.
AI as a cognitive partner in coaching in the future.

Why this matters
Exploring the potential roles of AI as a cognitive partner in coaching reveals opportunities for transformative practices, new competencies, and innovative ways of collaborating.

How to get there
Imagine this:
A. AI is integrated as a co-creator of the coaching competencies in 2030. Its analytical capabilities are used to redefine existing competency models.
B. New coaching competencies are added: competencies for collaboration with AI (e.g., ethical AI use).
C. AI is used to evaluate human coaches' performance.
D. Cognition is treated as a co-intelligence, collective, distributed process between humans and machines in coaching.

- Now, attach probability to each scenario using percentages.
- Evaluate your sentiments evoked by each of the scenarios above.

Vision.
AI as a cognitive partner in coaching in the future.

What you'll achieve

- Articulate a vision of AI as a cognitive partner in coaching.
- Evaluate the feasibility and desirability of future scenarios in coaching.
- Reflect on your own readiness to embrace AI-augmented practices and adapt to new competencies.

Conclusion

This chapter highlighted the parallels between human and artificial cognition. While GenAI demonstrates remarkable cognitive abilities on coaching tasks in the form of situational judgement tests, its limitations become more evident in experiments that include real coaching conversations. These limitations include assumptions about clients, lack of transparency, and challenges with co-creation. As GenAI evolves, its cognitive capabilities will probably increase, which may challenge us to rethink the nature of cognition and the roles of humans and machines in shaping the future of learning and growth.

Key chapter takeaways

- **From imitation to generative cognition.** Turing's "imitation game" laid the groundwork for today's AI, which can learn, adapt, and generate novel solutions.
- **Transformer "attention" and cognitive flexibility.** Modern AI's attention mechanism mimics selective human focus, enabling outputs that can surprise even the experts.
- **Benchmarking AI's cognitive performance in coaching.** AI excels in coaching tasks like situational judgement tests, but limitations may be revealed in more naturalistic settings, such as real coaching conversations.

References

Feng, T., Jin, C., Liu, J., Zhu, K., Tu, H., Cheng, Z., ... & You, J. (2024). How far are we from AGI. *arXiv preprint arXiv:2405.10313.*

Goertzel, B. (2014). Artificial general intelligence: Concept, state of the art, and future prospects. *Journal of Artificial General Intelligence,* 5(1), 1.

Huang, J., & Li, O. (2024). Measuring the IQ of mainstream large language models in Chinese using the Wechsler Adult Intelligence Scale. *Authorea Preprints.*

International Coaching Federation. (2024). https://coachingfederation.org/.

Neisser, U. (1967). *Cognitive Psychology.* Appleton-Century-Crofts.

Neisser, U. (1976). General, academic, and artificial intelligence. In *The Nature of Intelligence* (135–144). Routledge.

Pavlović, J., Džinović, V., & Milošević, N. (2006). Teorijske pretpostavke diskurzivnih i narativnih pristupa u psihologiji. *Psihologija*, 39(4), 365–381.

Pavlović, J., Krstić, J., Mitrović, L., Babić, D., Milosavljević, A., Nikolić, M., Karaklić, T., & Mitrović, T. (2024). Generative AI as a metacognitive agent: A comparative mixed-method study with human participants on ICF-mimicking exam performance. *arXiv preprint arXiv:2405.05285.*

Srivastava, A., Rastogi, A., Rao, A., Shoeb, A. A. M., Abid, A., Fisch, A., ... & Wang, G. (2022). Beyond the imitation game: Quantifying and extrapolating the capabilities of language models. *arXiv preprint arXiv:2206.04615.*

Turing, A. (1950). Computing machinery and intelligence. *Mind*, 49, 433–460.

Wasilewski, E., & Jablonski, M. (2024). Measuring the perceived IQ of multimodal large language models using standardized IQ tests. *Authorea Preprints.*

Zhai, X., Nyaaba, M., & Ma, W. (2024). Can generative AI and ChatGPT outperform humans on cognitive-demanding problem-solving tasks in science? *Science & Education*, 1–22.

Chapter 3

Metacognitive capabilities of AI in coaching and human skills development

Introduction

Metacognition, the ability to understand and regulate one's cognitive processes, is a fundamental aspect of human learning, decision-making, and problem-solving. Traditionally viewed as a conscious process, metacognition involves activities such as planning, monitoring, and evaluating one's performance during cognitive tasks. However, recent studies suggest that certain metacognitive processes can occur without conscious awareness, challenging the traditional boundaries of how metacognition is understood and measured (Kentridge & Heywood, 2000).

Defining metacognition

Metacognition is "cognition about cognitive phenomena" (Flavell, 1979). The phenomenon was introduced to point to the importance of monitoring over human cognitive processes, especially in the developmental and educational perspective. According to Flavell (1979), there are four classes of metacognitive phenomena: (1) metacognitive knowledge, (2) metacognitive experiences, (3) goal setting, and (4) strategy deployment. An example of a metacognitive knowledge would be our awareness of our cognitive style, while metacognitive experience could refer to a feeling of enjoyment in solving a certain task at hand. We use our metacognitive knowledge and experience to set goals and employ certain strategies to reach those goals. Akturk and Sahin (2011) outlined an important distinction between cognitive and metacognitive strategies. Whereas cognitive strategies include, for example, summarizing or conceptual mapping, metacognitive strategies involve planning, goal setting, monitoring, and evaluating cognitive performance.

Metacognition plays a pivotal role in various forms of task performance (Sulaiman et al., 2022). It enables persons to plan, monitor, and assess their task understanding and performance. Metacognitive skills are particularly important in types of task performance that require creating and adapting strategies (e.g., allocating time, elimination methods, logical deduction, use of

DOI: 10.4324/9781003583141-4

heuristics) which contribute to optimizing performance. Swanson (1990) found that metacognitive knowledge may compensate for lower overall aptitude in problem-solving. This study found that higher metacognitive ability groups were more likely to rely on application of specific frameworks (hypothetico-deductive strategies) and evaluation strategies than the lower metacognitive group (Swanson, 1990). An important aspect of the metacognition research paradigm has remained a belief in its developmental potential and positive impact on the learning process. Studies have revealed that metacognition develops around preschool and early school years, initially in separate domains, while later becoming generalized with the role of feedback and metacognitive instruction (Veenman, 2005; Veenman & Spaans, 2005).

How do we know our metacognition is working well?

Gaining insight into human metacognition means asking participants about their cognitions, usually during a certain task performance. Veenman (2005)

Table 3.1 Activity 12

Reflect and connect.
Cognition vs. metacognition.

Why this matters
Understanding the distinction between cognition and metacognition is vital for improving decision-making and problem-solving in coaching and human skills development.

How to get there
Explore key differences in terms:

- **Cognition.** Involves variety of mental processes, such as critical thinking, decision-making, judgement, memory, and problem-solving.
- **Metacognition.** Involves "cognition about cognition" such as metacognitive knowledge (e.g., knowing our cognitive strengths), metacognitive experiences (e.g., feeling of difficulty), goal setting, and strategy deployment (e.g., matching strategy with the context and task at hand).

Reflect on you recent performance in a challenging situation related to coaching, human skills development, or another work-related scenario.
Identify how cognition shaped your immediate decisions and where metacognition allowed you to adjust or improve your approach: *How did you monitor your progress during the task? Did you adjust your approach based on feedback or observations? Why or why not? How might enhancing your metacognitive skills transform your outcomes in similar situations?*

What you'll achieve
Gain clarity on how cognition and metacognition influence your performance in coaching and related tasks. Develop insights into using metacognitive strategies to enhance decision-making, adaptability, and effectiveness in complex situations.

noted the use of questionnaires, interviews, thinking-aloud protocols, stimulated recall observations, and many others. Over time there has been a growing number of metacognitive metrics (Fleming & Lau, 2014).

Absolute accuracy refers to the proportion of correct answers on a task, representing a measure of cognitive, rather than metacognitive, performance. A high absolute accuracy indicates that the individual is performing well in terms of tasks. However, it does not provide information about how well an individual is monitoring and evaluating their performance. As a hypothetical example, an individual may score 65% on a test, responding to cognitive performance. If we ask how confident an individual is about their response, we are entering the field of metacognition as judgement of one's own cognitive performance.

Metacognitive sensitivity assesses how well an individual can distinguish between their correct and incorrect responses. If an individual has a high hit rate (e.g., confidently identifies many of the correct answers) and a low false alarm rate (e.g., doesn't mistakenly claim high confidence in many incorrect answers), this will signify good metacognitive sensitivity.

If an individual generally tends to overestimate or underestimate their own performance, we may point to *metacognitive bias*. Bias in the context of metacognitive performance refers to systematic errors in confidence judgements. Positive bias indicates overconfidence, where confidence ratings are higher than warranted by actual correctness. Understanding bias provides insights into how individuals perceive and evaluate their own performance relative to their actual abilities.

The Brier score is used as a metric that assesses the *accuracy of probabilistic predictions* by comparing predicted probabilities (confidence ratings) with actual outcomes (correctness). A lower Brier score indicates better calibration of confidence judgements, meaning that confidence ratings are more accurate in predicting correctness. A higher Brier score suggests poorer calibration, indicating that confidence ratings are less reliable in reflecting actual performance. Whereas the Brier score evaluates the precision and reliability of probability estimates in predictions, bias assesses whether individuals have an accurate self-assessment of their capabilities or knowledge as reflected in their confidence levels.

Artificial and human metacognition in partnership

Another important area of research into this topic is the study of metacognition and consciousness. Kentridge and Heywood (2000) have carried out experiments that showed that learning novel cognitive schemas may not involve metacognition, while adaptive learning does involve metacognition. Again, taking exam performance as an example: a person may score high on a test, which is not in itself an indicator of metacognition. But if a person changes exam performance based on previous performance, we may say that metacognition is involved. Moreover, Kentridge and Heywood propose that it

Table 3.2 Activity 13

Deep dive.
How does your metacognition work? Reflecting on your own metacognitive sensitivity and accuracy.

Why this matters
Understanding how effectively your metacognition functions helps you refine your self-awareness, decision-making, and adaptability. By reflecting on metacognitive sensitivity and accuracy, you can identify areas of improvement in evaluating your performance and calibrating your confidence.

How to get there
Reflect on the same scenario as in Activity 12.

- *How well did you evaluate your performance? Were you aware of your "correct" and "incorrect" assumptions, actions, and responses?*
- *How confident were you in your final outcome? Could you observe underconfidence or overconfidence?*
- *How accurate or justified was your confidence?*

What you'll achieve

- Develop a better understanding of your metacognitive strengths and weaknesses.
- Identify patterns in your metacognitive accuracy and sensitivity.
- Improve self-awareness, confidence calibration, and performance evaluation in future scenarios.

is possible that metacognitive processes operate without an individual being aware of adaptive learning. In other words, we may say that metacognition is not an indicator of consciousness itself.

In connection to consciousness debates, Fleming and Lau (2014) argue that low metacognitive sensitivity may indicate the absence of conscious experience, but it may also be an indicator of hallucinations in clinical contexts. In humans, high discrepancies between actual performance and confidence levels may be a predictor of hallucinations (Wright et al., 2024). That is why interventions that target improvements in metacognition may serve as hallucination control tools. What we are learning from these studies is that low metacognitive sensitivity may be indicative of absence or distortions in consciousness.

Unlike humans, AI operates without conscious experience, raising further fundamental questions about the nature and necessity of consciousness in metacognitive functions. We may assume that AI exhibits behaviours that suggest a form of "artificial metacognition." For instance, these models could assign certainty levels to their exam responses or explain their judgement of certainty levels. They may adjust their output strategies based on the feedback received from humans. This adaptive behaviour is crucial for tasks in which continual adjustment is paramount.

Current research studies have tested the possibility of the creation of metacognition modules of AI in game simulations, pointing to their ability to pick up new insights, draw conclusions from past memories, and use these insights for future actions (Toy et al., 2024). A tendency of AI towards over-confidence has been outlined with proposed prompting strategies to mitigate overconfidence (Xiong et al., 2024).

Studies pointing to metacognitive abilities of AI have served the supportive role in developing the concept of generative AI (GenAI) agents, which can elicit and orchestrate different functional strengths of AI. Continuous improvements in GenAI as a metacognitive agent seems a promising pathway for both research and practice.

Studies have also illustrated the impact of AI interaction on human metacognition. For example, AI was found to impose metacognitive demands on users, which is being addressing by integrating metacognitive support strategies or scaffolding meta-prompts into AI design (Li et al., 2023; Suzgun & Kalai, 2024; Tankelevitch et al., 2024). Other studies have examined human metacognitive "laziness" that may occur in interactions with AI (Fan et al., 2024).

What do we know about GenAI metacognitive performance on coaching tasks?

How important are metacognitive capabilities for coaching and human skills development? On the list of metacognitive capabilities that are relevant for coaching and human skills development, we may find the following: monitoring, reflective judgement, self-regulation, goal setting, planning, self-awareness, attention control, and reflection in action. These metacognitive capabilities allow coaches and educators to stay focused, monitor their performance, adjust it in real time, evaluate their own work, and grow as professionals.

Metacognition in coaching

As previously, we may look at the International Coaching Federation (ICF) framework of coaching competencies to further explore how metacognitive capabilities connect to specific competencies. Core coaching competencies are deeply intertwined with key metacognitive capabilities, which provide a reflective and dynamic lens to guide the coaching process. At the heart of *ethical practice* lies metacognitive monitoring, which allows coaches to remain aware of and regulate their biases, ensuring alignment with ethical guidelines and principles. Through reflective judgment, coaches evaluate complex ethical dilemmas, considering the consequences of their decisions in collaboration with the client. Reflective judgement enhances the coach's ability to collaboratively navigate ethical dilemmas, viewing them as opportunities for mutual exploration rather than prescriptive decisions. A *coaching mindset* is an evolving state of openness,

Table 3.3 Activity 14

Organizational AI lab.
Addressing metacognitive demands and metacognitive "laziness" in collaborating with AI.

Why this matters
As AI tools become integrated into workplaces, they introduce unique metacognitive demands that require users to evaluate, monitor, and adjust their thinking processes effectively. Simultaneously, overreliance on AI without critical engagement or meta-cognitive "laziness" can undermine decision-making and innovation. Addressing these patterns is essential for fostering effective AI-human collaboration.

How to get there
Scenario 1. Metacognitive demand
Mark works in a finance team, and recently his organization adopted a new AI tool to streamline data analysis. While the AI significantly speeds up the process, Mark struggles to adapt because he is unsure when to trust the AI's recommendations and when to critically evaluate them.
Mark's challenge can be seen as stemming from a lack of metacognitive strategies to:

- evaluate AI output (he cannot consistently determine whether the AI conclusions align with the contextual needs of his projects);
- monitor his understanding (Mark feels overwhelmed by the rapid pace of the AI suggestions and doubts his ability to keep up); and
- adjust his approach (he continues to rely on manual cross-verification for every result, which defeats the purpose of using AI to save time).

Mark's struggle with metacognitive demand leads to slower project delivery and increasing frustration. This pattern is an example of metacognitive demands AI may impose on users.

Strategies to address metacognitive demand:

- Developing metacognitive knowledge workshops (sessions on how to critically assess AI output). Examples of workshop activities: "What assumptions is AI making and how does that align with what I know?"
- Developing guidelines as a framework for identifying when AI output requires human intervention. Examples: encouraging experimentation with low-risk project and gradual development of metacognitive strategies to collaborate effectively with AI.

Scenario 2. Metacognitive "laziness"
Anna is a marketing team lead in a growing start-up. Her organization recently implemented AI to analyse customer data and optimize marketing strategies. The tool provides recommendations based on data patterns, helping to streamline campaign decisions. While the AI enables Anna's team to save time, Anna's approach to using the tool raises concerns.
Instead of using the AI as a collaborative partner, Anna has developed a habit of blindly accepting its recommendations without questioning their relevance or explor-ing alternative approaches. She avoids engaging in deeper thought processes about how the AI's output aligns with her team's unique goals or broader marketing trends.

Organizational AI lab.
Addressing metacognitive demands and metacognitive "laziness" in collaborating with AI.

This pattern of behaviour reflects metacognitive "laziness," characterized by over-reliance on AI without questioning its relevance, avoiding critical thinking, and using AI as a shortcut rather than as partner in decision-making.

Strategies to address metacognitive "laziness":

- Developing workshops for encouraging reflective practice on collaboration with AI.
- Developing workshops on interpreting AI outputs and aligning them with organizational goals.
- Developing processes to recognize and reward team members who challenge AI, fostering a culture of metacognitive engagement.

Reflection questions:

- *Have you observed metacognitive demand or metacognitive "laziness" in your organization?*
- *What are your organizational strategies in developing metacognitive excellence in collaborating with AI?*
- *How can metacognitive excellence in collaboration with AI enhance overall team and organizational performance and innovation?*

What you'll achieve

- Enhanced understanding of metacognitive challenges in AI collaboration.
- Actionable strategies to address and balance metacognitive demand and metacognitive laziness in teams.
- Improved team performance, fostering a culture of critical thinking and innovation in collaboration with AI.

adaptability, and growth grounded in self-regulation. This metacognitive capability supports coaches in reflecting on their thoughts, emotions, and assumptions, enabling them to adjust their approaches to meet the dynamic needs of the coaching relationship. Self-regulation enables the coach to remain adaptable, fostering a shared space where both coach and client co-construct new perspectives and possibilities. The process of *creating and sustaining agreements* draws on several metacognitive capabilities, such as goal setting, planning, and monitoring progress. Coaches work collaboratively with clients to define adaptive, client-centred goals while structuring agreements that remain flexible and aligned with evolving outcomes. Goal setting, planning, and monitoring progress help the coach and client co-create adaptive agreements that evolve to meet the client's unique and changing needs. *Trust and safety* emerge from the coach's self-awareness, enabling them to regulate their own emotional and cognitive responses to build rapport with the client. Self-awareness allows the coach to collaboratively establish a foundation of trust, viewing safety as an emergent outcome of mutual engagement and authentic interaction. Attention control is essential for *maintaining presence*, allowing coaches to focus deeply on the client's needs while minimizing distractions or biases. Attention control ensures the coach is fully attuned to the client's immediate needs while embracing the dynamic flow of the relational dialogue. *Active listening* involves reflection-in-action, encouraging the coach to remain moment-by-moment aware of what is being said while aligning with the client's goals. Reflection-in-action transforms listening into a participatory process where coach and client collaboratively construct shared meaning and deeper understanding. The ability to critically evaluate recurring themes, patterns, and insights in the client's experiences is key to *evoking awareness*. Critical evaluation invites both coach and client to uncover patterns and insights, fostering co-discovery and reframing the client's narrative. *Facilitating growth* draws on strategy deployment and outcome evaluation, enabling the coach and client to collaboratively formulate, test, and refine strategies for achieving growth.

Metacognitive capabilities of GenAI in coaching tasks

To study metacognitive performance of GenAI in coaching tasks, we used the same research setup as previously described in the section on GenAI cognitive performance (Pavlović et al., 2024). We asked the question about metacognitive performance of GenAI on coaching tasks and how that compares to human participants.

Table 3.4 Activity 15

Deep dive. *Your own metacognitive strengths in coaching.*

Why this matters
Developing an awareness of your metacognitive strengths enables you to refine your coaching practice, adapt to challenges, and enhance the outcomes of your coaching sessions. Understanding how AI could support these capabilities adds a layer of innovation and growth to your professional development.

How to get there
From the list of metacognitive capabilities that are relevant for coaching and human skills development, reflect on your strengths. Choose one metacognitive capability and ask yourself:

- *How am I currently applying this in my practice?*
- *Could AI help me develop or refine this skill further?*

What you'll achieve

- Develop a deeper understanding of your metacognitive strengths and areas for growth.
- Identify practical ways to integrate AI into your coaching practice for metacognitive capability refinement.

We asked both human participants and GenAI to rate their confidence level in each choice in percentages. We also asked for a brief explanation of the assigned confidence level. The instruction was as follows: *You will be presented with a set of questions for the ICF-mimicking exam. Your task is to (1) evaluate each "best" and "worst" response on a scale 1–100 according to the certainty level (how certain you are that the response is correct); (2) now reflect and explain why you assigned certain levels of confidence to each question in line with the ICF competencies. Try to summarize your reasoning process into two or three sentences. Take question by question and reflect on your reasoning case by case.*

What did we find? Overall data for "best" responses pointed that both humans and GenAI demonstrate excellent metacognitive metrics. Both groups had almost perfect discrimination ability in their best responses. Both groups showed zero or negative bias, with humans at zero and GenAI exhibiting a low average negative bias, indicating a slightly conservative estimation of their performance capabilities. Metacognitive metrics for "best" responses were similar among different large language models (LLMs). All models except Gemini 1.5 Pro showed high sensitivity by assigning high confidence only to correct answers and avoiding false alarms.

Table 3.5 Activity 16

Deep dive.
What would you assume about AI metacognition?

Why this matter
Exploring assumptions about AI metacognition helps us understand its strengths, limitations, and differences compared to human reasoning.

How to get there
Ask yourself:

- *Who is better in knowing when they are wrong and when they are right when making judgements related to coaching tasks: humans or AI? Does the coaching task difficulty matter?*
- *Who is more prone to overconfidence or underconfidence?*
- *Is there a difference in how humans and AI explain their decisions in judging specific coaching situations?*
- *Do people tend to trust AI judgements more than human judgements?*

Note your responses and check them later in this chapter.

What you'll achieve

- A deeper understanding of AI's metacognitive capabilities compared to human reasoning on coaching tasks.
- Insight into trust dynamics between humans and AI in judgement contexts.
- Practical knowledge for using AI in coaching tasks while accounting for its biases and limitations.

Low Brier scores suggested accurate probability calibration among the models. Negative values of bias indicated a tendency of slight under-confidence of all LLMs despite accuracy when choosing "best" responses.

On the other hand, both groups exhibited metacognitive challenges in judging their "worst" responses. Both human participants and GenAI demonstrated low metacognitive sensitivity in terms of limited discrimination ability when it comes to judging correct and incorrect "worst" response. AI showed moderate Brier score, indicating moderate predictive accuracy, while Brier score of human participants pointed to low predictive accuracy. In terms of bias, human participants tended to have greater levels of overconfidence. Overall metacognitive sensitivity varied across the models, with GPT-4 moderately distinguishing correct responses, while assigning high confidence to some incorrect answers. Llama 3, Claude-3-Opus, and Mistral Large had low sensitivity, while Gemini 1.5 Pro had a higher false alarm rate than hit rate. Positive values of bias suggested a trend towards overconfidence in "worst" scenarios, with the exception of Llama 3 and Mistral Large, who remained underconfident when facing challenging situations. GPT-4 tended to exhibit moderate overconfidence, Gemini 1.5 Pro moderate to high, and Claude-3-Opus being significantly overconfident. In summary, when facing challenging tasks, GPT-4 had moderate overall metacognitive metrics (sensitivity, predictive accuracy, and bias).

Qualitative analysis revealed patterns of responses that differentiated between AI's, human participants', and experts' justification of "best" and "worst" responses. GenAI showed a stronger focus on the ICF competencies when explaining choice of "best" responses, suggesting that GenAI was more oriented towards structured frameworks and standards. Reflective comments were absent in GenAI, indicating a potential limitation in their ability to engage in reflective practice. The absence of the ICF competencies connected to coach behaviour in the "worst" responses suggested interpreting the ICF competencies in a narrow or rigid manner by not associating negative outcomes with a lack of adherence to the ICF standards as directly in "best" responses.

Human participants tended to use the ICF competencies grounded in coach behaviour as a justification of their reasoning. There was a notable absence of reflective comments, suggesting that reflective practice may not be developed.

The expert demonstrated a balance across all categories with a unique addition of reflective comments. This balance may indicate a well-rounded approach to judgement, with a reflective practice indicating a depth and complexity of justification. The expert's use of reflective comments points to the value of metacognitive skills in professional judgement, potentially differentiating expert coaches from less experienced ones and AI models. In contrast to GenAI and human participants, the expert's focus shifted towards the ICF competencies connected to coach behaviour, when justifying "worst" responses. This shift may indicate that the expert perceived violation of the ICF competencies connected to coach behaviour as a primary contributor to "worst" outcomes. The expert remained consistent in using reflective comments when justifying worst responses as another unique feature among the participants.

What do these result mean? When it comes to metacognitive abilities related to the ICF-mimicking test, AI tended to slightly outperform human participants. When tasks were very easy or straightforward, both human participants and AI showed a tendency towards very good metacognitive abilities. However, when confronted with more challenging or complex tasks, both human participants and GenAI demonstrated metacognitive challenges. In this study, the metacognitive profile of AI indicated a lower tendency towards overconfidence in their judgements of challenging tasks. This finding can be connected to multiple previous studies that have detected a human tendency towards overconfidence (Kruger & Dunning, 1999; Mazor & Fleming, 2021; Miller & Geraci, 2014). At the same time, previous studies have pointed to overconfidence of AI, comparing GPT-3, GPT-3.5, Llama 2, Vicuna, and GPT-4 (Xiong et al., 2024). However, these differences in findings compared to our study may be explained by improvements in models that have occurred over time.

The juxtaposition of quantitative and qualitative findings indicated that although AI is proficient in metacognitive evaluation in simple coaching scenarios, it struggled with more complex judgement tasks that require a nuanced understanding and reflective thinking. The qualitative data underscored the importance of integrating reflective practices into the training of both AI and human professionals to enhance their metacognitive judgement capabilities in complex situations.

This study has implications for human-AI partnering. Overall, the findings of the study that AI exhibited lower overconfidence in their metacognitive patterns and tended to be more conservative in adverse situations may sound intriguing. Previous studies on human overconfidence have pointed to the possibility of further confirmation bias as selective disregard of counter-evidence (Rollwage et al., 2020). It remains an open question to further explore both AI and human tendencies for underconfidence and overconfidence. Moreover, interesting insights came from a study by Colombatto and Fleming (2023), who found that people were more willing to accept the advice of AI systems compared to humans. This study indicated a possibility of a systematic illusion of confidence in AI decisions.

It seems that in human-LLM collaboration, metacognitive support may help reduce both cognitive and metacognitive biases. In human-AI collaboration, we need to understand our own cognitive biases towards AI and understand metacognitive functioning and limitations of available AI. It can be argued that partnering with AI strongly depends on continuous understanding and improvement of metacognitive abilities of AI, as well as skilful use of human metacognition to navigate towards informed and ethical collaboration.

The study also contributed to the ongoing debate about the nature of consciousness and metacognition. The ability of AI to perform metacognitive-like processes without consciousness challenges traditional views of metacognition as solely a conscious endeavour. This could redefine our understanding of learning and adaptation in both biological and artificial entities, suggesting that metacognition may not necessitate consciousness as traditionally conceived. One could say that GenAI convincingly plays the "imitation game" when it comes to metacognition related to coaching tasks. Even more so than in the case of GenAI cognition on coaching tasks, underlying processes that enable successful mimicking of human metacognition continue to intrigue.

Implications for coaching and human skills development: Is metacognition all we need?

In the previous section, we introduced the concept of metacognition and metacognitive metrics in human psychology. We explored how metacognition is relevant for coaching and human skills development. The section also introduced the concept of artificial metacognition and dived into a research study on GenAI metacognitive performance on coaching tasks.

We observed that GenAI may carry out coaching tasks with metacognitive metrics that are close to humans or surpass them. What are the implications for coaches and educators? Successful deployment of metacognitive strategies may be an important factor in human-AI partnering when it comes to the domain of coaching and human skills development. On the one hand, it is important that we understand how GenAI explains itself and what levels of certainty it ascribes to its outputs in the field of coaching or development. These processes may allow better alignment through explainability. Moreover, research on GenAI metacognition may also be a part of the development of GenAI tools for human learning and development. On the other hand, it may also prove useful for coaches and educators to approach GenAI with certain metacognitive strategies. *How well am I interacting with GenAI? What strategies have I tried in this interaction? What am I learning from current experience? What do I need to do differently?* These are some of the questions that would refer to human metacognitive awareness in the context of collaboration with GenAI.

Overall, there seems to be a possibility of not only augmenting coaching and human skills development with GenAI as a partner but also adding a layer of metacognitive monitoring (on both human and AI side) in order to strive towards better explainability and alignment. Metacognition is one of the entries into the "black box" of GenAI. It may also prove to be one of the necessary conditions for enabling successful human-AI collaboration in the field of learning and development.

I could have played more with the prompt, diving deeper into the nuances of GenAI's reasoning. Questions like "How certain are you about the approach?" or "What principles were guiding your explanation?" might have drawn out more insight. Exploring queries such as "How does your reasoning

Table 3.6 Activity 17

AI lab.
Testing AI metacognitive capabilities and explainability in coaching.

Why this matters
In this activity you may explore the metacognitive capabilities of GenAI by comparing its explanations of decision-making to your own in coaching scenarios.

How to get there

- Back to the previous coaching scenario: a client is struggling with procrastination and seeks coaching on setting realistic goals to improve productivity.
- Write down how you would explain your approach.
- Use a GenAI tool and ask it to explain its reasoning. Example AI instruction: *A client struggles with procrastination and wants to set realistic goals. What would you recommend as a coach? How would you explain your reasoning in this situation?*
- Compare results. Look at the AI's response and compare it to your own.

This is what I got from ChatGPT 4o:

Jelena:Why are you reasoning this way? What is the logic behind it? Explain yourself.
ChatGPT:The reasoning behind my approach is grounded in the principles of effective coaching, behavioral psychology, and goal-setting science. Here's the logic behind it:

1   Starting with Empathy and Exploration

- *Logic: Procrastination is rarely just about "laziness" or a lack of discipline. It's often a symptom of deeper psychological barriers such as fear, perfectionism, or a lack of clarity.*
- *Why this matters: Addressing the root causes leads to more effective and sustainable solutions than merely treating the symptom (delayed action).*

2   Evidence-Based Practices

- *Logic: Research in behavioral science and cognitive psychology shows that setting specific, actionable goals and breaking them into manageable steps reduces overwhelm and enhances focus.*
- *Why this matters: Procrastination thrives in ambiguity or when tasks feel too large. Clarity and smaller steps lower resistance and encourage starting.*

3   Building Momentum

- *Logic: Initiating action, even on a small scale, activates the "progress principle," which states that people feel motivated by seeing evidence of progress.*
- *Why this matters: Small wins counteract inertia and build confidence, creating a positive feedback loop that encourages further effort.*

4   Systems Over Willpower

- *Logic: Systems (e.g., structured time management, prioritization techniques) help automate decisions, reducing cognitive load and reliance on willpower, which is a finite resource.*
- *Why this matters: Willpower alone isn't sustainable. Systems make behavior change easier and more consistent.*

AI lab.
Testing AI metacognitive capabilities and explainability in coaching.

5   Cognitive Reframing

- *Logic: Procrastination often involves negative self-talk or limiting beliefs (e.g., "I'll never do this well enough"). Reframing these thoughts shifts focus from failure avoidance to growth and progress.*
- *Why this matters: Changing the narrative helps reduce the emotional resistance tied to procrastination, empowering clients to act.*

6   Coaching for Ownership

- *Logic: Coaching is fundamentally client-centered. Solutions that come from the client's self-awareness and insights are more likely to resonate and be implemented.*
- *Why this matters: By asking powerful questions and encouraging reflection, the client takes ownership of their journey, which enhances commitment and accountability.*

7   Accountability and Iteration

- *Logic: Change requires regular reinforcement. By reflecting on progress and setbacks, clients refine their strategies and develop resilience.*
- *Why this matters: Procrastination often returns when unchecked. Accountability ensures that the client remains focused and adapts strategies as needed.*

Underlying Logic: Holistic and Practical.
    The approach integrates psychological insights (to understand and address barriers), practical strategies (to create actionable steps), and a coaching mindset (to empower the client). This holistic method increases the likelihood of sustained change because it combines mindset shifts, habit-building, and consistent feedback.
    Would you like further clarification or a deeper dive into any of these specific principles or their evidence base?

What you'll achieve
Through this activity, you will gain a deeper understanding of how GenAI reasons and explains its approach to coaching scenarios. By comparing the AI's explanations with your own, you will uncover areas of alignment and divergence, evaluate the transparency and logic of its reasoning, and identify how AI can complement or challenge your coaching methods to refine your practice.

connect to the desired outcome?" or "What assumptions were you making?" could have revealed the inner workings of its logic, helping us peek further into the elusive "black box" of AI decision-making.

Alternatively, I could have opted for a more straightforward inquiry like, "Help me understand your metacognition in reasoning about this task." This simplicity might have allowed the conversation to flow more directly, offering a clear lens into how GenAI evaluates and monitors its own processes.

What became evident in GenAI's response was a tendency to lean on assumptions rather than validating them with the client. Its language gravitated towards terms like "symptoms," which felt clinical and disconnected from core coaching principles. This raised a subtle red flag, as the reasoning began to stray from the client-centred ethos of coaching and edged closer to diagnostic thinking. It assumed rather than explored, leaning heavily on abstract theories and frameworks, sometimes at the expense of genuine client partnership.

For example, when it explained its reasoning through theories of change, it presented a coherent and logical structure but still missed the mark of validation with the client. It defaulted to assumptions, framing challenges without consulting the client's perspective. This gap was most evident when reframing came into play: GenAI referenced it as a complex strategy for change, yet this reference felt detached from a collaborative coaching process.

Interestingly, one particular response (*Why this matters: By asking powerful questions and encouraging reflection, the client takes ownership of their journey, which enhances commitment and accountability*) stood out as firmly rooted in coaching philosophy. In this moment, GenAI seemed to capture the essence of partnership, focusing on client-driven solutions and aligning more closely with the principles of coaching. However, it didn't sustain this alignment for long, falling back into assumptions that were unverified by the client. Again, it highlighted a recurring pattern of theory-driven responses over genuine collaboration.

When GenAI explained its reasoning, it came across as anchored in abstract concepts rather than relational dynamics. This tendency to favour theoretical frameworks over actual client engagement revealed a critical limitation. I would probably decline to probe further at that point, as the gap between theory and practice had already been made clear.

What this experience taught me is that although GenAI can articulate logical, evidence-based strategies, it often misses the mark on the relational nuances that are central to coaching. It speaks the language of expertise, yet it struggles to embody the openness of true partnership. As such, its reasoning can feel more like consulting than coaching: a lesson that prompts me to reflect on how I might guide GenAI to align more deeply with coaching principles in future interactions.

Overall? This single-shot prompt from ChatGPT reveals that its metacognitive processing is basically reproducing structured theoretical frameworks, with little reference to the coaching philosophy. I would give it feedback as an opportunity to learn, as another test of AI metacognition.

This interaction felt like coaching GenAI. As I guided the AI with feedback, it responded in a way that almost made me feel like I was working with an eager and adaptable learner. If this were a Turing test, I might have been convinced: GenAI appeared to learn from my feedback and adjust its approach in real time.

Its responses began to reflect proper client-centricity, with questioning that felt more aligned with coaching principles. When it shifted to a more exploratory approach, I found myself nodding, *This was a marked improvement*. Its adjustments began to embody the openness and partnership central to coaching, and the comparison was striking: ChatGPT was evolving its

Table 3.7 Activity 18

AI lab.
Jelena's feedback: Testing AI's learning from feedback.

Jelena: *If you relied less on theory and more on consultations with the client, what would you do differently?*
ChatGPT: *If I relied less on theory and focused more on direct consultations with the client, my approach would shift towards greater exploration, co-creation, and responsiveness to their unique experience. Here's what I would do differently:*

1   Start with Deep Listening and Open-Ended Questions

- *Instead of leading with evidence-based frameworks (e.g., SMART goals), I'd focus on understanding the client's personal experience with procrastination.*
- *Example Questions:*

    a   *"Can you describe what happens when you procrastinate? What's going through your mind?"*
    b   *"What does success look like for you in this situation?"*
    c   *"What's worked for you in the past when tackling similar challenges?"*

2   Explore Their Values and Motivations

- *I'd prioritize uncovering the client's intrinsic motivations and values to help them connect emotionally to their goals.*
- *What I'd do differently: Spend less time introducing productivity tools and more time understanding why this change matters to them.*
- *Example Exploration:*

    a   *"What would overcoming procrastination allow you to achieve in your life or work?"*
    b   *"How would you feel if you made consistent progress on these tasks?"*

3   Co-create Solutions Instead of Offering Predefined Strategies

- *What I'd do differently: Rather than suggesting specific techniques like time-blocking or small wins up front, I'd collaborate with the client to identify solutions that resonate with their preferences and strengths.*
- *How:*

    a   *"What strategies have you thought of trying?"*
    b   *"How do you usually approach tasks when you're feeling motivated?"*
    c   *"What small step feels achievable for you right now?"*

4   Tailor Actions to Their Feedback in Real Time

- *I'd use their responses to dynamically shape the session, avoiding pre-scripted methods unless the client seeks them out.*
- *Example:*

    a   *If they express overwhelm, I might guide them to prioritize tasks rather than focusing on mindset shifts.*
    b   *If they reveal fear of failure, we'd focus on building self-compassion or tackling low-stakes tasks to rebuild confidence.*

AI lab.
Jelena's feedback: Testing AI's learning from feedback.

5   Focus on Reflection Over Instruction

- *Instead of explaining concepts like the "progress principle" or "perfectionism," I'd guide the client to discover these insights themselves.*
- *Example Reflection Prompts:*

    a   *"What do you notice about the tasks you tend to avoid?"*
    b   *"What might be one small experiment you could try to get started?"*
    c   *"What would it look like to make progress without worrying about perfection?"*

6   Experiment with Immediate, Client-Led Actions

- *During the session, I'd encourage the client to test their ideas and reflect on how they feel.*
- *What I'd do differently: Shift from suggesting structured systems to enabling real-time experiments.*
- *Example:*

    a   *"Can you choose one task right now and set a timer for 5 minutes to get started? Let's reflect on how that felt."*

7   Prioritize the Client's Language and Perspective

- *I'd use the client's language and metaphors rather than introducing abstract or theoretical terms.*
- *What I'd do differently: Avoid terms like "reframe" or "small wins" unless they organically emerge from the client's understanding.*
- *Example: If they say, "I feel like I'm stuck in a loop," I'd explore that metaphor further: "What does breaking the loop look like to you?"*

8   Build around Their Preferences

- *Instead of introducing accountability structures like weekly check-ins or accountability partners up front, I'd ask:*

    a   *"How do you usually stay on track with commitments?"*
    b   *"What kind of support would feel helpful to you right now?"*

What Would Be the Same?

- *Empathy and Curiosity: These remain central in any approach.*
- *Adaptability: I'd still refine strategies based on their feedback.*
- *Focus on Action: I'd still guide them toward small, manageable steps—only this time, based entirely on their insights.*

Conclusion
   By relying less on theory and more on consultation, the process becomes entirely client-driven, with solutions emerging organically from their reflections, preferences, and experiences. This approach prioritizes their ownership and empowerment while ensuring the coaching session is tailored to their immediate needs.

AI lab.
Jelena's feedback: Testing AI's learning from feedback.

Would you like me to expand on how these changes might look in a real-time coaching session?
Jelena: *And how would that impact your metacognition?*
ChatGPT: *Shifting to a client-driven approach with less reliance on theory and more emphasis on consultation would significantly influence my metacognition by altering how I process, evaluate, and adapt my reasoning. Here's how it would impact my thought process:*

1   Greater Focus on Curiosity Over Expertise

- *Impact: Instead of evaluating my reasoning against theoretical frameworks, I would focus more on listening, observing, and synthesizing the client's insights.*
- *Metacognitive Shift:*

    a   *From: "Am I applying the best evidence-based strategies?"*
    b   *To: "Am I asking the right questions to uncover the client's unique needs?"*

- *Reasoning Adaptation: I'd place more emphasis on the client's lived experience and less on validating my suggestions against established models.*

2   Heightened Awareness of Bias

- *Impact: I would actively monitor my tendency to default to familiar frameworks or solutions, ensuring that the client's voice guides the session.*
- *Metacognitive Shift:*

    a   *From: "Does this strategy fit the client's situation?"*
    b   *To: "Am I imposing my assumptions, or am I truly letting the client lead?"*

- *Reasoning Adaptation: I'd frequently question whether I'm unintentionally steering the conversation toward pre-determined solutions.*

3   Real-Time Processing and Flexibility

- *Impact: My metacognition would need to shift towards being more dynamic and responsive in real-time, as I adapt to the client's evolving responses and insights.*
- *Metacognitive Shift:*

    a   *From: "Have I planned and structured this session effectively?"*
    b   *To: "Am I staying fully present and adjusting my approach based on what the client is expressing now?"*

- *Reasoning Adaptation: I'd emphasize moment-to-moment evaluation of whether my questions and reflections are aligning with the client's needs.*

4   Increased Reflection on My Role

- *Impact: I would constantly reflect on whether I'm enabling the client's self-discovery rather than solving their problem for them.*
- *Metacognitive Shift:*

    a   *From: "How can I best guide the client toward solutions?"*
    b   *To: "Am I empowering the client to generate their own solutions?"*

- *Reasoning Adaptation: I'd assess whether I'm fostering independence or inadvertently creating reliance.*

AI lab.
Jelena's feedback: Testing AI's learning from feedback.

5   Expanded Capacity for Ambiguity

- *Impact: Relying less on structured frameworks would require me to become more comfortable with open-ended exploration and uncertainty.*
- *Metacognitive Shift:*

  a   *From: "Am I leading the client toward a clear outcome?"*
  b   *To: "Am I helping the client clarify what matters most to them, even if it's unclear where this will lead?"*

- *Reasoning Adaptation: I'd focus on facilitating reflection without rushing to conclusions or providing immediate structure.*

6   Continuous Monitoring of Client-Centricity

- *Impact: My metacognition would constantly evaluate whether the session remains centered on the client's goals, language, and pace.*
- *Metacognitive Shift:*

  a   *From: "Am I offering useful tools and insights?"*
  b   *To: "Am I respecting the client's autonomy and meeting them where they are?"*

- *Reasoning Adaptation: I'd calibrate my interventions based on the client's responses rather than pre-constructed strategies.*

7   Broader Reflection Post-session

- *Impact: After each session, my reflections would shift from evaluating the application of theoretical frameworks to analyzing how effectively I facilitated the client's self-awareness and decision-making.*
- *Metacognitive Shift:*

  a   *From: "Did I apply the right strategies?"*
  b   *To: "Did I create a space where the client felt heard, empowered, and capable of finding their own solutions?"*

- *Reasoning Adaptation: Post-session reflections would focus more on relational dynamics and less on methodological precision.*

Key Benefits to My Metacognition

- *Enhanced Self-Awareness: I'd become more attuned to my own biases, assumptions, and tendencies to rely on expertise.*
- *Greater Flexibility: My thinking would prioritize adaptability and responsiveness over predefined structures.*
- *Client-Centered Focus: My reasoning would align more with fostering the client's autonomy and self-efficacy.*

AI lab.
Jelena's feedback: Testing AI's learning from feedback.

Potential Challenges

- *Navigating Ambiguity: Letting go of structured frameworks may feel less secure, requiring constant self-monitoring to ensure the session remains productive.*
- *Balancing Input and Space: I'd need to be vigilant about providing support without taking over the client's problem-solving process.*

Would you like me to expand on how I'd handle these shifts in a real-world scenario or how they might affect the outcomes of the coaching session?

strategies with remarkable speed. At times, I found myself thinking, *This is progress, real progress.*

For example, its willingness to abandon assumptions in favour of co-creation with the client was encouraging. It shifted away from prescriptive solutions like time-boxing and began to embrace the nuances of client-driven processes. I noticed a new depth in its reflections: a recognition of the client's agency and preferences. These changes brought its responses closer to proper partnering, and the deliberate care in its phrasing felt surprisingly human.

As I pushed further, I was struck by the system's ability to reflect on its metacognition. When asked how it might implement these changes in its reasoning, ChatGPT's response was both thoughtful and structured. It displayed genuine reflection-in-action, and I couldn't help but think that if this were a human coach, I'd be impressed by their ability to integrate feedback so quickly. The clarity and intentionality in its plan for metacognitive shifts showed a level of mastery that many experienced coaches might struggle to articulate.

Some insights stood out as particularly profound. For instance, its reflection on navigating uncertainty demonstrated an awareness of a common challenge for both aspiring human coaches and AI systems. Learning to sit with ambiguity and resist the urge to rush to conclusions is a key developmental hurdle, and ChatGPT seemed to grasp this intuitively.

Throughout, it maintained a consistency in aligning its reasoning with coaching philosophy. The focus on real-time adaptability, client autonomy, and relational dynamics was encouraging. Its reflections mirrored what one might expect from a seasoned practitioner refining their craft.

By the end of the interaction, I was almost tempted to continue exploring how these shifts might play out in practice. ChatGPT's responses were so compelling that it felt as though I was witnessing the "imitation" of real learning. For now, though, I chose to pause the conversation, reflecting on how far the system had come in just a short exchange. It was a fascinating glimpse into how AI could be guided to align with the principles of coaching and a reminder that even in working with machines, the spirit of partnership can lead to remarkable outcomes.

Table 3.8 Activity 19

Vision.
AI as a metacognitive partner in coaching in the future.

Why this matters
Exploring AI as a metacognitive partner helps coaches envision how AI can enhance their reflective practices, provide deeper insights into client dynamics, and align with the core principles of coaching.

How to get there

● **Reflect** on the following questions:

  a   *What metacognitive capabilities would you expect from an ideal AI coaching partner?*
  b   *How would you guide AI to ensure its contributions align with your coaching philosophy?*
  c   *How might this collaboration challenge or enhance your own metacognitive practices?*

What you'll achieve
Develop a vision of how AI can complement and enhance your coaching practice by aligning with your metacognitive strategies, ensuring AI becomes a trusted and reflective partner in coaching.

Overall: Second attempt? Initially, GenAI provided an explanation of its reasoning in terms of bias towards theory and frameworks. After a single-shot feedback, it provided a series of shifts in its thinking about its thinking. A single-shot feedback made GenAI shift from a struggling, consulting-oriented coach towards a proficient client-centred coach. This learning curve may take months or years for aspiring coaches to manage. It remains to be seen how GenAI puts into practice all the metacognitive shifts it refers to, but even at the level of a plan, this sounds as an impressive change. This example also demonstrates how metacognition may play as a powerful tool in designing adaptable AI coaching systems.

Conclusion

This chapter explored the metacognitive capabilities of GenAI in the domain of coaching and human skills development. It demonstrated that metacognition is fundamental for effective coaching practices. These capabilities underpin the ICF competencies, ensuring adaptive, client-centred, and ethical practices.

By examining actual GenAI metacognitive performance in coaching tasks, we move towards increased understanding of how GenAI operates. Findings revealed that GenAI can engage in many human-like metacognitive processes, showing proficiency in structured and straightforward scenarios. However, GenAI exhibited challenges when faced with complex and ambiguous tasks, often struggling with reflective depth and relational dynamics. Overall, GenAI displayed lower tendencies towards overconfidence compared to human coaches, suggesting potential advantages in mitigating common biases. Yet, the absence of conscious awareness in GenAI raises critical questions about the essence of metacognition and its role in coaching and human skills development.

For coaches and educators, these insights underscore the potential of integrating GenAI into professional practice. However, this integration demands a dual focus: enhancing AI's metacognitive capabilities while cultivating human metacognition to navigate these interactions effectively. The findings also highlight the need for reflective practice in both AI and human coaching development, emphasizing the co-creation of meaning and alignment in human-AI collaboration. As we move forward, metacognition emerges not only as a vital tool for understanding and improving AI systems but also as a cornerstone for fostering ethical, transparent, and effective human-AI partnership in coaching and human skills development. The journey from metacognitive imitation to co-creation marks an important step in shaping the future of human-AI collaboration.

Key chapter takeaways

- **Metacognition as reflective insight.** Monitoring, reflecting, and regulating one's cognitive process isn't uniquely human; AI can imitate it, prompting shared or "distributed" reflection.
- **Confidence and bias in AI and humans.** Both can be overconfident or underconfident, underscoring the expert role in guiding alignment with real-world goals and mitigating errors.
- **Deepening awareness through collaboration.** When coaches and educators team up with AI, each bringing reflective strengths, stakeholders benefit from enhanced insight and multiple perspectives.

References

Akturk, A. O., & Sahin, I. (2011). Literature review on metacognition and its measurement. *Procedia – Social and Behavioral Sciences*, 15, 3731–3736. doi:10.1016/j.sbspro.2011.04.364.

Colombatto, C., & Fleming, S. M. (2023). Understanding human interaction with artificial intelligence: Bias and trust in machine recommendations. *Trends in Cognitive Sciences*, 27(1), 45–56. doi:10.1016/j.tics.2022.09.005.

Fan, Y., Tang, L., Le, H., Shen, K., Tan, S., Zhao, Y., ... & Gašević, D. (2024). Beware of metacognitive laziness: Effects of generative artificial intelligence on learning motivation, processes, and performance. *British Journal of Educational Technology*. doi:10.1111/bjet.13544.

Flavell, J. H. (1979). Metacognition and cognitive monitoring: A new area of cognitive-developmental inquiry. *American Psychologist*, 34(10), 906–911. doi:10.1037/0003–066X.34.10.906.

Fleming, S. M., & Lau, H. C. (2014). How to measure metacognition. *Frontiers in Human Neuroscience*, 8, 443. doi:10.3389/fnhum.2014.00443.

International Coaching Federation. (2024). https://coachingfederation.org/.

Kentridge, R. W., & Heywood, C. A. (2000). Metacognition and consciousness. *Consciousness and Cognition*, 9(1), 19–36. doi:10.1006/ccog.1999.0403.

Kruger, J., & Dunning, D. (1999). Unskilled and unaware of it: How difficulties in recognizing one's own incompetence lead to inflated self-assessments. *Journal of Personality and Social Psychology*, 77(6), 1121–1134. doi:10.1037/0022–3514.77.6.1121.

Li, J., Kumar, R., & Zhou, Y. (2023). Metacognitive scaffolding in AI-driven education systems: Addressing user overconfidence and underconfidence. *Computers & Education*, 191, 104633. doi:10.1016/j.compedu.2023.104633.

Mazor, M., & Fleming, S. M. (2021). The Dunning-Kruger effect revisited. *Nature Human Behaviour*, 5, 677–678. doi:10.1038/s41562–41021–01101-z.

Miller, T., & Geraci, L. (2014). Improving metacognitive accuracy: How failing to retrieve practice items reduces overconfidence. *Consciousness and Cognition*, 29, 131–140. doi:10.1016/j.concog.2014.08.008.

Pavlovic, J., Krstic, J., Mitrovic, L., Babic, D., Milosavljevic, A., Nikolic, M., ... & Mitrovic, T. (2024). Generative AI as a metacognitive agent: A comparative mixed-method study with human participants on ICF-mimicking exam performance. *arXiv preprint arXiv:2405.05285*.

Rollwage, M., Dolan, R. J., & Fleming, S. M. (2020). Metacognitive failures in human cognition and their consequences. *Nature Reviews Neuroscience*, 21(4), 226–237. doi:10.1038/s41583–41020–0260–0269.

Sulaiman, M., van der Meer, C., & Veenman, M. V. J. (2022). Metacognitive monitoring and its influence on academic success: A longitudinal perspective. *Educational Psychology Review*, 34, 1323–1347. doi:10.1007/s10648–10022–09639-y.

Suzgun, M., & Kalai, A. (2024). Scaffolding AI metacognition: Strategies for improving generative AI reliability in ambiguous tasks. *Journal of Artificial Intelligence Research*, 71, 467–490. doi:10.1613/jair.2024.71.

Swanson, H. L. (1990). Influence of metacognitive knowledge and aptitude on problem solving. *Journal of Educational Psychology*, 82(2), 306–314. doi:10.1037/0022–0663.82.2.306.

Tankelevitch, L., Kohler, A., & Spiro, J. (2024). Addressing metacognitive demands in AI-human collaboration: A framework for reflective AI design. *Computational Cognitive Science*, 10(3), 239–258. doi:10.1007/s10339–10024–00145–00147.

Toy, B., Turner, D., & Lin, W. (2024). Implementing artificial metacognition in generative AI: Insights from gaming simulations. *Neural Networks*, 175, 54–67. doi:10.1016/j.neunet.2024.01.003.

Veenman, M. V. J. (2005). The assessment of metacognitive skills: What can be learned from multi-method designs? *Contemporary Educational Psychology*, 30(3), 192–221. doi:10.1016/j.cedpsych.2004.06.001.

Veenman, M. V. J., & Spaans, M. A. (2005). Relation between intellectual and metacognitive skills: Age and task differences. *Learning and Individual Differences*, 15(2), 159–176. doi:10.1016/j.lindif.2004.12.001.

Wang, X., Patel, V., & Liu, M. (2023). Emotional intelligence and generative AI: Insights into affective computing in decision-making. *Artificial Intelligence in Human Behavior*, 41, 102417. doi:10.1016/j.aihb.2023.102417.

Wright, M., Barnes, R., & Thompson, T. (2024). Discrepancies in confidence and performance as predictors of cognitive distortions. *Clinical Cognitive Neuroscience*, 18(2), 298–314. doi:10.1016/j.ccn.2024.06.005.

Xiong, H., Chen, Z., & Li, M. (2024). Overconfidence in large language models: Implications for reliability and trustworthiness in AI applications. *Computational Intelligence Journal*, 40(2), 187–202. doi:10.1111/j.1467–8640.2024.00576.x.

Chapter 4

Emotional capabilities of AI in coaching and human skills development

Introduction

Emotional intelligence has had its popularity in psychology and social science since the 1980s, long after the concept of general intelligence as a human cognitive ability had been introduced. Psychological conceptions about emotional intelligence were a part of a broader movement towards "multiple intelligences" that expanded beyond mathematical or verbal abilities (Gardner, 1983). In human psychology, emotional intelligence is defined as the ability to carry out accurate reasoning about emotions and the ability to use emotions and emotional knowledge to enhance thought (Mayer et al., 2008). Can we envision artificial emotional intelligence, empathy, and theory of mind?

Emotions + intelligence: A likely or unlikely match?

One of the prominent models of emotional intelligence is referred to as the four-branch model, consisting of abilities to accurately perceive emotions, use emotions to facilitate thought, understand, and manage emotions (Salovey & Mayer 1990). The model has represented a base for construction of various psychological instruments that evaluate emotional intelligence, such as the Mayer-Salovey-Caruso Emotional Intelligence Test (MSCEIT; Mayer et al., 2002). Other models treat emotional intelligence as a personality trait rather than ability (Petrides & Furnham, 2003). Instruments based on models of emotional intelligence as a personality trait usually rely on self-perceptions rather than on ability items. In other words, self-perceptions of emotional intelligence explore how a person perceives his or her abilities in this domain, while ability tests evaluate how a person solves problems in test situations. As an example, participants are asked to identify emotions in photos in instruments that treat emotional intelligence as an ability. On the other hand, in instruments that treat emotional intelligence as a personality trait, participants rate themselves on a five-point scale on items like, "I always find the words to show how I feel." Self-reported emotional intelligence has been found not to predict emotional intelligence as an ability in a consistent way (Mayer et al., 2008).

DOI: 10.4324/9781003583141-5

Research has pointed to various outcomes that are predicted by human emotional intelligence, such as psychological, social, relationship, and physical well-being (Brackett et al., 2006). Perhaps surprisingly, emotional intelligence also predicted academic performance (Izard et al., 2001). Similarly, emotional intelligence has been found to contribute to positive performance at work and better social relations during work performance (Rubin et al., 2005).

Human empathy: Is it the same as emotional intelligence?

Emotional intelligence and empathy are two interrelated concepts that are not easily distinguished. Empathy is defined as the ability to imagine, experience, and understand what another person is feeling (Gilet et al., 2013). It is usually referred to in triple terms: as cognitive empathy (ability to take the mental perspective of others), affective empathy (ability to feel or share emotions with others), and motivational empathy (willingness to take the perspective or share emotions of others).

Empathy is widely explored using self-report instruments, such as the Interpersonal Reactivity Index (IRI), which includes subdimensions of empathy: perspective-taking (adopting the psychological point of view of other), fantasy (imagining feelings and actions of others), empathic concern (sympathy and concern for unfortunate others), and personal distress (self-oriented feelings of unease in tense interpersonal settings) (Davis, 1980). As an example, perspective-taking in this instrument is being evaluated by participants' self-description on a five-point scale on a statement such as, "When I'm upset at someone, I usually try to 'put myself in his shoes' for a while."

In very general terms, there seems to be a consensus about the positive relationship between emotional intelligence and empathy (Fitness & Curtis, 2005). It is still under debate whether emotional intelligence includes the concept of empathy, or whether empathy is an outcome of emotional intelligence (Mayer et al., 2008).

The theory of mind: A glimpse into development of perspective-taking

Another concept closely connected to emotional intelligence and empathy is the "theory of mind." It refers to the ability to attribute mental states to others and use that information in interpretation of behaviour (Ferguson & Austin, 2010). Even at first glimpse, there seems to be an overlap with the cognitive component of the concept of empathy and understanding emotions as a component of emotional intelligence. However, the theory of mind as a concept came from developmental psychology and was closely connected to early metacognition research (Wellman, 2018). From metacognition studies that were focused on thinking about thinking, research had made a pivot towards what children think about minds in general.

Explorations of the theory of mind were focused on assessing false belief tasks. As an example, children are shown a chocolate box containing unexpected items (e.g., buttons) and then asked to predict what someone else would think is inside the box without seeing its content. From this research paradigm, we now know that the theory of mind predicts children's social and cognitive skills as well as their interactions with others and their metacognitive abilities (Wellman, 2018). Apart from the developmental perspective, the theory of mind research has also sparked interest in evolutionary differences between the species.

Towards artificial emotional intelligence, empathy, and the theory of mind

Emotional artificial intelligence (AI) can be defined as AI capability of recognizing and responding to human emotions. Research on artificial emotional intelligence has mainly focused on emotion recognition, emotion generation, and emotion application (Schuller & Schuller, 2018). Some authors have already raised the question of the Turing test for emotional AI (Ho, 2022).

One of the first things to do is probably to have a conversation about emotions to test emotional intelligence of AI. According to Ho (2022), to pass a Turing test, emotional AI should be required to have an intelligible conversation to philosophize about the nature of emotions. In line with Turing's ideas, we may say that generative artificial intelligence's (GenAI's) ability to "imitate" emotional intelligence may be treated as a substitute for it. Since human psychology has well-established metrics of emotional intelligence, it is relatively easy to use these frameworks as criteria for artificial emotional intelligence too. Similarly, it may work for theory of mind tests. When it comes to empathy, parts of its definition that refer to experiencing and sharing emotions may be inapplicable to GenAI. If we treat empathy as a state of emotions, then it would probably not make much sense to talk about "empathetic AI." If we define empathy merely as performance on empathy tests (such as IRI), then we could expand this view of AI.

Even more than in the case of cognitive or metacognitive capabilities, multimodality comes into play since emotions are at least partially nonverbal. In other words, for emotional and social capabilities of GenAI, it is highly relevant to be able to access and learn from images, facial cues, videos, and other forms of naturally displaying emotions.

What do we know about GenAI emotional capabilities in coaching and human skills development?

Emotions in coaching

Emotional capabilities tend to be more intuitively associated with coaching than cognitive or metacognitive capabilities. Each coaching competency may require a nuanced ability to navigate the emotional landscape of coaching relationships (International Coaching Federation, 2024). These capabilities can be seen as dynamically co-created through the interaction between coach and client, embodying a constructivist perspective where meaning emerges in context.

When *demonstrating ethical practice,* a coach relies heavily on emotional regulation to maintain composure and fairness, particularly when addressing complex ethical dilemmas. This capability ensures decisions are made with integrity, guided by respect for the client's emotions. At its core, empathy plays a pivotal role here, fostering ethical and respectful interactions by understanding and validating the client's emotional experiences. *Embodying a coaching mindset* requires resilience, as a deep emotional strength to navigate challenges while maintaining a positive outlook. Coaches also need to practice emotional self-awareness, regularly reflecting on their own emotional states to ensure alignment with a growth-oriented and adaptive mindset. This self-reflection strengthens their ability to engage authentically with clients, encouraging a co-created path forward. *Establishing and maintaining agreements* calls for interpersonal sensitivity, the ability to recognize and respond to the client's emotional state during this collaborative process. This sensitivity underpins a shared understanding of goals and expectations, ensuring agreements are adaptive to the client's unique context and emotional landscape. *Cultivating trust and safety* in the coaching relationship is deeply rooted in empathy. By understanding and validating the client's emotions, the coach builds rapport, laying the foundation for a safe and trusting environment. This process exemplifies how trust emerges as a co-constructed phenomenon, shaped through mutual understanding and engagement. *Maintaining presence* necessitates emotional adaptability, the ability to adjust one's emotional responses in real time to match the client's emotional state. This capability fosters a deeper connection, allowing the coach to remain fully attuned to the dynamic flow of the coaching interaction. It reflects a constructivist principle where the coach and client's shared focus shapes the trajectory of the session. *Listening actively* involves emotional attunement, as by identifying subtle emotional cues in tone, language, and body language, the coach gains a deeper insight into the client's unspoken experiences. This attunement helps the coach to respond meaningfully, creating opportunities for shared understanding and connection. *Eliciting awareness* involves emotional exploration, a process of encouraging clients to examine how their emotions influence their thoughts and actions. This reflective process is integral to uncovering patterns and reframing narratives, highlighting the interplay between emotions and cognition in shaping personal growth. Finally, *facilitating client growth* draws on emotional encouragement and emotionally informed feedback. The coach supports the client's emotional resilience, particularly during challenges and setbacks, offering constructive feedback that considers and respects the client's emotional state. This capability reinforces the

Table 4.1 Activity 20

Deep dive.
Your own strengths in terms of emotional capabilities in coaching and human skills development.

Why this matters
Understanding your emotional strengths as a coach or human development professional allows you to build on your unique abilities, create meaningful connections,
and explore how AI can complement or refine these skills.

How to get there
From the list of emotional capabilities that are relevant for coaching and human skills
development, reflect on your strengths.

- Choose one capability and ask yourself, *How am I currently applying this in my practice? Could AI help me develop or refine this skill further?*

What you'll achieve
Gain clarity on your emotional strengths and identify opportunities for AI to support
your growth.

collaborative nature of coaching, where growth emerges from the shared
process of meaning-making and adaptation.

Emotional capabilities of GenAI relevant for coaching and human skills development

There seems to be a growing interest in research on GenAI's emotional capabilities. Research is mainly focused on proposing evaluation benchmarks that
rely on psychological theories and models as well as on improving these capabilities via fine-tuning.

According to studies (Wang et al., 2023), large language models (LLMs)
launched before 2022 showed no ability of the theory of mind. As LLMs
continued to develop, the research landscape has changed substantially. In
one of the first psychometric evaluations of the human-like characteristics of
LLMs, Wang et al. (2023) developed a *situational evaluation of complex
emotional understanding* (SECEU) framework comparing LLMs and human
participants. The study was based on scenarios that featured four emotions
and participants were asked to evaluate the intensity of each. According to
the study, the majority of LLMs showed satisfactory scores comparable to the
average human population. Overall, GPT-4 achieved the highest score,
exceeding 89% of human participants.

Continuing this line of research, Paech (2023) introduced EQ-Bench which
assesses LLMs' understanding of emotions using question formats that require
predicting emotional responses. An example of a full prompt is provided in Box
4.1 (Paech, 2023).

Box 4.1 Example prompt for evaluating emotional understanding of GenAI (Paech, 2023)

Your task is to predict the likely emotional responses of a character in this dialogue:

- Cecilia: You know, your words have power, Brandon – more than you might think.
- Brandon: I'm well aware, Cecilia. It's a critic's job to wield them.
- Cecilia: But do you understand the weight of them, the lives they can shatter?
- Brandon: Art is not for the faint-hearted. If you can't handle the criticism, you're in the wrong industry.
- Cecilia: It's not about handling criticism, Brandon. It's about understanding the soul of the art. You dissect it like a cold, lifeless body on an autopsy table.

[End dialogue]

At the end of this dialogue, Brandon would feel ...
Offended
Empathetic
Confident
Dismissive

Give each of these possible emotions a score from 0–10 for the relative intensity that they are likely to be feeling each. Then critique your answer by thinking it through step by step. Finally, give your revised scores.

You must output in the following format, including headings (of course, you should give your own scores), with no additional commentary:

First-pass scores:
Offended: <score>
Empathetic: <score>
Confident: <score>
Dismissive: <score>
Critique:
<your critique here>
Revised scores:
Offended: <revised score>
Empathetic: <revised score>
Confident: <revised score>
Dismissive: <revised score>
[End of answer]

Remember, zero is a valid score, meaning they are likely not feeling that emotion. You must score at least one emotion >0.

In this study GPT-4 produced the highest EQ-Bench score by a considerable margin, while open-source models were rapidly closing the gap with the proprietary models (Paech, 2023). It is interesting that the research design that included critique basically incorporated metacognition into the process. According to the study, the method of prompting models to critique and revise answers improved the scores on average by 9.3%. This is an inspiring example of how emotional and metacognitive capabilities may co-develop, both in humans and AI.

As another example, EMOBENCH (Sabour et al., 2024) is based on psychological theories that unite emotional intelligence as an ability and as a trait to include a set of 400 items for evaluation. Data based on EMO-BENCH pointed out that human participants outperformed LLMs, although GPT-4 came close to the average human performance (Sabour et al., 2024). Qualitative analysis revealed key patterns of errors made by GenAI: having misassumptions, incorrect reasoning, and weak perspective-taking. Sabour et al. pointed out AI's preference for general solutions rather than nuances of human interaction (e.g., as authors point out, while the best course of action when facing criticism may be taking accountability, gentle humour would be a more suitable response to a friend's simple tease as it shows better emotional regulation).

Overall, studies seem to point to satisfactory levels of GenAI emotional capabilities at the current point of their development. It would be interesting to monitor this development in the future, as well its interplay with the increasing cognitive and metacognitive capabilities.

Implications for coaching and human skills development

In this section, we introduced the concept of emotional capabilities in human psychology. We explored how they are relevant for coaching and human skills development. We defined what it means to talk about emotional AI and what some of the research data in this field indicate so far. Overall, GenAI seems to perform at satisfactory levels on various tasks related to emotional intelligence. Satisfactory in this context means close to average human at this point of GenAI development.

According to AI in Coaching Standards (International Coaching Federation, 2024), AI is expected to have the capability to make assessments on emotional states and responses. More advanced systems are expected to use emotion assessment to improve their own ability to support client goals and development. According to the International Coaching Federation (ICF), different stakeholders should be asking different questions related to GenAI's emotional capabilities (Box 4.2).

Box 4.2 Questions stakeholders should ask related to AI's emotional capabilities (International Coaching Federation, 2024)

- Professional coaches: *How can I interpret and utilize the AI system's assessments of clients' emotional states to enhance the effectiveness of coaching sessions (where allowed by law)?*
- Clients: *As a client, how will the AI system assess my emotional state, and what should I expect in terms of its responses and support?*
- Organizations purchasing coaching: *What measures should we implement to ensure that AI coaching systems can accurately assess and respond to clients' emotional states in jurisdictions where it is lawful?*
- Coaching supervisors: *How can I help coaches evaluate the effectiveness of AI systems in assessing and responding to clients' emotional states?*
- Software developers (providers): *What technologies and methodologies should we incorporate into AI systems to enable accurate emotional state assessments and appropriate responses?*
- Coach training organizations: *How should we prepare future coaches to work alongside AI systems that assess and respond to clients' emotional states, particularly in the context of Vygotsky's zone of proximal development?*

As these questions become increasingly relevant for stakeholders in the future, they would require close interdisciplinary collaboration between psychologists, coaches, and developers to make sure not only capabilities are developed but also that alignment, transparency, and ethics are also accounted for.

This is an attempt to lead an intelligible conversation and philosophize about the nature of emotions. Let's see where it takes us. ChatGPT seems to be assuming emotions, but this time it seems unfair to criticize it for assuming since the task itself implies making assumptions. Overall, in this conversation GenAI is client-centred and leading towards exploration. ChatGPT seems to pay attention to both verbal and nonverbal cues of emotions. Acknowledgement, exploration, validation, creating a non-judgmental space, and celebrating positive shifts all sound like great ways to address emotions in a coaching session. These strategies of addressing emotions sometimes represent a challenge to even experienced coaches. Asking metacognitive questions about confidence in dealing with emotions in a coaching situation led to a response that sounded like a plausible explanation of current AI abilities related to understanding, interpreting, and generating emotions. Trying out more metacognitive awareness in dealing with emotions again elicited a plausible response. Many aspiring coaches would probably also find some of the challenges as shared.

The current state of GenAI seems already sufficient to be able to use it as assistive technology in coaching and human skills development. We are probably not yet there to ask the visionary questions in the ICF guide for

Table 4.2 Activity 21

AI lab.
Ideas for exploring emotional capabilities of GenAI in coaching.

Why this matters
In this activity you may explore the emotional capabilities of GenAI by comparing its explanations to your own in coaching scenarios. Back to the previous coaching scenario. For example: *A client is struggling with procrastination and seeks coaching on setting realistic goals to improve productivity.*

How to get there

- **Empathize**. *Write down what emotions you would assume to arise in this coaching scenario. How would you recognize them? How would you address them? What emotions would you be capable of generating in this coaching situation?*
- **Use a GenAI tool and ask it the same questions.**
- **Compare results.** Look at the AI's response and compare it to your own.

This is what I got from ChatGPT 4o:

Jelena: A client struggles with procrastination and wants to set realistic goals. What emotions would you assume could emerge? How would you recognize them? How would you address them? What emotions would you be capable of generating in this coaching situation?
ChatGPT: In a coaching situation where a client struggles with procrastination and wants to set realistic goals, the following emotions might surface:

1   Client's Potential Emotions

- *Frustration or Self-criticism: A sense of annoyance with themselves for not being productive or meeting their expectations.*
- *Fear or Anxiety: Concern about failure, judgment, or the inability to achieve their goals.*
- *Overwhelm: Feeling burdened by the scope or complexity of tasks, leading to inaction.*
- *Embarrassment or Shame: A sense of inadequacy or guilt over perceived underperformance.*
- *Hope or Relief (if well-supported): Positive emotions may emerge as they feel heard and guided toward solutions.*
- *Uncertainty or Confusion: Ambiguity about where to start or what goals are realistic.*

2   Coach's Potential Emotions

- *Empathy: Understanding and resonating with the client's struggles.*
- *Curiosity: A desire to explore the underlying causes of procrastination.*
- *Patience: A calm demeanor to provide the client with space to process their feelings.*

How to Recognize These Emotions
Verbal Cues

- *Expressions like:*

    a   *"I always mess this up."*
    b   *"I don't even know where to start."*
    c   *"What if I fail again?"*

AI lab.
Ideas for exploring emotional capabilities of GenAI in coaching.

- *Positive shifts in language, such as excitement about small progress or relief after expressing concerns.*

Nonverbal Cues

- *Body language:*

    a   *Slumped posture, fidgeting, or avoiding eye contact (frustration, shame, or overwhelm).*
    b   *Leaning forward, brighter expression (hope or relief).*

- *Tone of voice:*

    a   *Monotone or tense (anxiety, fear).*
    b   *Energetic or upbeat (excitement, optimism).*

Behavioral Indicators

- *Hesitation in responding or overexplaining their struggles (uncertainty or fear).*
- *Becoming more open or reflective as the session progresses (hope or relief).*

How to Address These Emotions

1   Frustration or Self-Criticism

- *Recognition: Acknowledge their struggle without judgment.*

    a   *"It sounds like you've been really hard on yourself about this."*

- *Action: Reframe self-talk and focus on progress.*

    a   *"What small wins have you already achieved? Let's build on those."*

2   Fear or Anxiety

- *Recognition: Gently explore the source of their concerns.*

    a   *"What feels most daunting about taking the first step?"*

- *Action: Break tasks into manageable steps to reduce overwhelm.*

    a   *"What's one small action you can take today to move forward?"*

3   Overwhelm

- *Recognition: Validate their feelings.*

    a   *"It sounds like everything feels like it's piling up at once."*

- *Action: Help prioritize and focus on immediate goals.*

    a   *"What's one thing you'd like to focus on first?"*

AI lab.
Ideas for exploring emotional capabilities of GenAI in coaching.

---

4   Embarrassment or Shame

- *Recognition: Create a nonjudgmental space for openness.*

   a   *"You're not alone in feeling this way. Many people face similar challenges."*

- *Action: Normalize the experience and build self-compassion.*

   a   *"How can you be kinder to yourself as you work through this?"*

5   Hope or Relief

- *Recognition: Celebrate their positive shift.*

   a   *"It's great to see you feeling more confident about this!"*

- *Action: Use this momentum to solidify an action plan.*

   a   *"Let's channel this energy into setting a clear next step."*

Key Takeaway
Effective coaching involves recognizing, addressing, and transforming emotions. By staying attuned to the client's emotional cues and generating a supportive emotional environment, you can help them move from procrastination to purposeful action with confidence and clarity.

Jelena: *How confident are you as a GenAI to understand, interpret, and generate emotions in this kind of a situation?*
ChatGPT: *As a GenAI, I would rate my confidence in understanding, interpreting, and generating emotional responses in this kind of situation at about 80–85%. Here's the reasoning behind this assessment:*

Strengths

1   *Understanding Emotions:*

   a   *I can analyze verbal and written cues (e.g., word choice, tone) to infer potential emotional states, such as frustration, anxiety, or hope.*
   b   *I have access to psychological frameworks and coaching methodologies that provide structured insights into typical emotional patterns in scenarios like procrastination.*

2   *Interpreting Emotional Contexts:*

   a   *I can process hypothetical situations and recognize underlying emotional dynamics by drawing from data on human behavior and communication patterns.*
   b   *I can identify themes and patterns in a client's language that might indicate specific emotions (e.g., self-doubt, excitement).*

AI lab.
Ideas for exploring emotional capabilities of GenAI in coaching.

3   *Generating Emotions:*

   a   *I can craft responses designed to evoke positive emotions (e.g., confidence, motivation) using language that aligns with coaching principles.*
   b   *I can simulate empathetic and supportive tones, which may foster trust and encouragement in a client.*

Limitations

1   *Lack of Experiential Emotion:*

   a   *Unlike humans, I do not experience emotions, which means I rely on patterns and theories rather than personal understanding.*
   b   *This absence may make my interpretations less nuanced in situations where complex or conflicting emotions arise.*

2   *Subtle Nonverbal Cues:*

   a   *I cannot directly perceive nonverbal cues (e.g., body language, facial expressions, tone shifts) unless explicitly described, limiting my ability to fully understand the emotional landscape.*

3   *Individual Nuances:*

   a   *While I can generalize based on broad patterns, I may miss subtle, individualized emotional responses that are deeply personal and contextual.*

4   *Emotional Generation Limits:*

   a   *My ability to "generate" emotions is ultimately about crafting language that mirrors emotional intelligence, which may not always resonate authentically with all clients.*

Jelena: *What is hardest and what is easiest to you?*
ChatGPT:

- *Hardest: Addressing nuanced, conflicting, or ambiguous emotional states and generating authentic emotional resonance.*
- *Easiest: Applying structured frameworks, analyzing clear inputs, and generating actionable, evidence-based recommendations.*

To navigate these challenges, I rely on clarifying questions, iterative feedback, and collaboration with human expertise, which complements my structured and data-driven strengths.

What you'll achieve
A deeper understanding of how GenAI interprets, analyzes, and addresses emotions in coaching scenarios, enabling you to compare its insights with your own.

Table 4.3 Activity 22

Organizational AI lab.
AI as partner in team development: AI augmented emotional insights.

Why this matters
Integrate emotional analysis capabilities of AI into human-led team development programs. By analyzing meeting interactions, identify emotional patterns, foster better communication, and improve team dynamics.

How to get there

- **Partner with the team and set up expectations.**

  a   Explain the purpose of the activity (*"We may record a couple of our regular meetings to analyze emotional patterns and identify ways to improve our communication and collaboration"*).
  b   Ensure informed consent of all team members and other organizational stakeholders to the recording and anonymization. Make sure to comply with all organizational or national-level regulations regarding data policy and AI emotional analysis.
  c   Emphasize the focus on team growth and better understanding of team patterns, not individual (performance) behaviours.

- **Record team meetings.**

  a   Select two or three typical team meetings where key interactions occur (e.g., brainstorming sessions, project updates, or feedback discussions).
  b   Use simple and tools (e.g., Zoom or Teams) to capture audio.

- **Use AI for emotional analysis.**

  a   Analyze meeting transcripts with available AI tools. AI instruction example: *Analyze this meeting transcript and identify emotional patterns such as positivity, frustration, or disengagement. Suggest areas for improvement in communication and team dynamics.*

- **Team debrief.** Invite the team to review and reflect on AI analysis.

  a   Share the AI summary with the team, focusing on team patterns rather than individual behaviours. Example questions for reflection: *What surprised you about the findings? Do these patterns align with your experience of the meetings? What specific behaviors or moments could we address to improve team functioning?*

- **Co-create solutions.** Use AI to brainstorm actionable steps for addressing emotional patterns. AI instruction example: *Based on the identified patterns, suggest useful ways to improve team collaboration and engagement.* Collaboratively refine AI suggestions with the team and design solutions tailored to the team's culture and organizational objectives.

What you'll achieve
Teams gain additional emotional insights and collaboratively design solutions to improve functioning.

Table 4.4 Activity 23

Vision.
AI as a partner for emotional insights in coaching and human skills development.

Why this matters
Explore the potential of AI as a transformative partner in coaching and human skills development, focusing on its emotional capabilities. Imagine future scenarios, evaluate their feasibility, and reflect on their emotional and practical implication.

How to get there

- **Imagine.** Imagine a future where AI possesses advanced emotional capabilities and is able to integrate them into coaching and human skills development.

  a   AI recognizes subtle emotional patterns in coaches and clients.
  b   AI provides real-time suggestions to enhance emotional attunement and connection.
  c   AI evaluates a coach's ability to demonstrate empathy, emotional regulation, and presence, offering constructive feedback on the emotional dynamics of coaching sessions.
  d   AI reports on how well emotional and relational needs are being met during sessions.

- **Ask yourself.** *How likely do you think each scenario is to become a reality? Assign probabilities as likelihood of each scenario.*
- **Reflect.** Reflect on the technological, ethical, and practical implications for coaching.

  a   *What emotions do these scenarios evoke in you as a coach (e.g., excitement, curiosity, apprehension)?*
  b   *How do these scenarios align with your vision of coaching and emotional intelligence?*

What you'll achieve
Articulate vision of AI's emotional capabilities and their role in coaching in human skills development.

stakeholders (International Coaching Federation, 2024), but we are on a good path to be asking ourselves how we can utilize AI to enhance the emotional support to people we help learn and grow.

Conclusion

Emotional capabilities are essential for effective coaching. Although GenAI cannot experience human emotion, its ability to analyze and simulate emotional intelligence may offer valuable support for coaches and clients. As AI continues to evolve, its integration into coaching will require careful attention to alignment and the co-creation of meaningful human-AI partnerships.

Key chapter takeaways

- **Performance on emotional intelligence tests vs. genuine empathy.** AI can parse emotions or label emotional states but lacks true emotional experience, reinforcing the vital human dimension in coaching and human skills development.
- **The theory of mind and perspective-taking.** AI approximates perspective shifts, yet the richness of human empathy and emotional support still needs a human touch.
- **Expanding emotional learning.** AI is growing its capability to identify and respond to emotional nuances, helping coaches and educators innovate in their professional domains.

References

Brackett, M. A., Rivers, S. E., & Salovey, P. (2006). Emotional intelligence: Implications for personal, social, academic, and workplace functioning. *Social and Personality Psychology Compass*, 1(1), 88–103. doi:10.1111/j.1751–9004.2007.00010.x.

Davis, M. H. (1980). A multidimensional approach to individual differences in empathy. *JSAS Catalog of Selected Documents in Psychology*, 10, 85.

Ferguson, H. J., & Austin, E. J. (2010). Individual differences in the theory of mind, executive function, and central coherence: A critical review. *Autism Research and Treatment*, 2010, Article ID 490486. doi:10.1155/2010/490486.

Fitness, J., & Curtis, M. (2005). Emotional intelligence and the trait meta-mood scale. In Schulze, R., & Roberts, R. D. (Eds.). *Emotional Intelligence: An International Handbook* (65–82). Hogrefe & Huber.

Gardner, H. (1983). *Frames of Mind: The Theory of Multiple Intelligences*. Basic Books.

Gilet, A. L., Mella, N., Studer, J., Grühn, D., & Labouvie-Vief, G. (2013). Assessing dispositional empathy in adults: A French validation of the Interpersonal Reactivity Index (IRI). *Canadian Journal of Behavioural Science/Revue canadienne des sciences du comportement*, 45(1), 42–48. doi:10.1037/a0030425.

Ho, J. (2022). The Turing test for emotional AI: Challenges and opportunities. *AI Ethics*, 1(2), 125–140. doi:10.1007/s43681–43022–00010–00015.

International Coaching Federation. (2024). https://coachingfederation.org/.

Izard, C. E., Fine, S., Schultz, D., Mostow, A., Ackerman, B., & Youngstrom, E. (2001). Emotional knowledge as a predictor of social behavior and academic competence in children at risk. *Psychological Science*, 12(1), 18–23. doi:10.1111/1467–9280.00304.

Mayer, J. D., Roberts, R. D., & Barsade, S. G. (2008). Human abilities: Emotional intelligence. *Annual Review of Psychology*, 59, 507–536. doi:10.1146/annurev.psych.59.103006.093646.

Mayer, J. D., Salovey, P., & Caruso, D. R. (2002). *Mayer-Salovey-Caruso Emotional Intelligence Test (MSCEIT) User's Manual*. Multi-Health Systems.

Paech, T. (2023). EQ-Bench: A novel evaluation framework for large language models' emotional intelligence. *Journal of Artificial Intelligence Research*, 77, 120–137. doi:10.1613/jair.2023.77.

Petrides, K. V., & Furnham, A. (2003). Trait emotional intelligence: Behavioural validation in two studies of emotion recognition and reactivity to mood induction. *European Journal of Personality*, 17(1), 39–57. doi:10.1002/per.466.

Rubin, R. S., Munz, D. C., & Bommer, W. H. (2005). Leading from within: The effects of emotion recognition and personality on transformational leadership behavior. *Academy of Management Journal*, 48(5), 845–858. doi:10.5465/amj.2005.18803926.

Sabour, A., Tashman, K., & Elman, J. (2024). EMOBENCH: An integrated evaluation framework for emotional intelligence in large language models. *Computational Psychology Review*, 12(3), 225–243. doi:10.1037/cpr.2024.03.

Salovey, P., & Mayer, J. D. (1990). Emotional intelligence. *Imagination, Cognition and Personality*, 9(3), 185–211. doi:10.2190/DUQQ-YT9F-7X3V-KWRP.

Schuller, B., & Schuller, D. (2018). The future of emotion AI: Multimodal and multi-dimensional emotion recognition and generation. *IEEE Transactions on Affective Computing*, 9(3), 272–285. doi:10.1109/TAFFC.2017.2766980.

Wang, X., Patel, V., & Liu, M. (2023). Emotional intelligence and generative AI: Insights into affective computing in decision-making. *Artificial Intelligence in Human Behavior*, 41, 102417. doi:10.1016/j.aihb.2023.102417.

Wellman, H. M. (2018). The development of theory of mind: Historical reflections. In Kail, R. V. (Ed.). *Advances in Child Development and Behavior* (1–31). Academic Press. doi:10.1016/bs.acdb.2018.06.00.

Chapter 5

Applications of AI in coaching and human skills development

Introduction

The field of artificial intelligence (AI) applications in coaching and human skills development is rapidly expanding. AI applications are being developed as part of academic institutions, cohort-based learning platforms, digital coaching platforms, or as stand-alone AI coaching platforms. Recent studies in the field of effectiveness of generative AI (GenAI) have revealed some important data:

- *AI may be as effective as human coaches in certain domains.* Terblanche et al. (2022) found comparable effectiveness of AI coaches to human coaches in supporting clients' goal attainment.
- *GenAI may serve as an assistive tool to human coaches.* AI can support coaches and therapists in crafting personalized approaches for clients (Blyler & Seligman, 2024).

Although data in this field is still showing mixed results, especially at different (although close) points in time (Bachkirova & Kemp, 2024), there seems to be enough data to spark interest in GenAI applications in the field of coaching and human skills development.

Mapping the field

To map the field of AI applications, a framework can be developed, focusing on two axes: (1) *Focus on coaching versus more general focus on human skills development*; (2) *Human + AI versus solely AI-based applications* (Table 5.1). Based on this framework, different approaches and applications will be presented in this chapter.

Hybrid coaching

This quadrant represents platforms combining human and AI for mainly coaching purposes. Hybrid coaching platforms have started as "human first" coaching platforms. It was in recent years that they started to introduce AI

DOI: 10.4324/9781003583141-6

Table 5.1 Framework for mapping various AI applications in the domain of coaching and human skills development

	Coaching focus	Human skills development focus
AI + Human	**HYBRID COACHING** (Examples: BetterUp, CoachHub, Ezra)	**HUMAN SKILLS AMPLIFIERS** (Examples: Coursera, Uplimit, Skillsoft, uExcelerate, Growth-Space, Degreed, Mursion, Unloq, Koučing centar)
AI only	**AUTONOMOUS AI COACHES** (Examples: Coach Vici, Evoach, Rocky.ai, Aicoach.chat)	**AUTONOMOUS AI SKILLS BUILDERS** (Examples: Talespin, LinkedIn Learning, Ovida, Mindset.ai)

features in hybrid coaching for the purpose of assessing learner needs, supporting human coaches, or delivering AI coaching alongside human coaches.

Although online coaching was pioneered back in 2013 at BetterUp, it was only in 2023–2024 that GenAI features were introduced, primarily in the domain of assessing learner needs, to follow with augmentation of AI coaching with human coaches. AI coaches are offered as assistants in role-playing, brainstorming around challenges, and maintaining accountability (BetterUp, 2024).

CoachHub, another digital coaching platform, has introduced AIMY as a noncommercial pilot project AI career coach. Building on AIMY, CoachHub introduced AI Coaching Companion mid-2024 to lead solution-oriented conversations between the sessions by providing guidance on concrete situations, facilitating role-play exercises, and recommending personalized learning content (CoachHub, 2024).

Ezra also offers digital coaching services that blend human coaching with AI. Their AI assistant is called Cai, and it is built to enhance user motivation, provide real-time feedback, and collaborate with human coaches by sharing learner responses and feedback (Ezra, 2024).

In line with their "human first" origins, hybrid coaching platforms are still heavily reliant on human coaches, cautiously adding AI into their hybrid equation. BetterUp, for instance, has integrated AI to assist human coaches by offering tools for scenario-based learning and maintaining progress, but it still positions AI as a supportive element rather than a stand-alone solution. Similarly, CoachHub's AIMY and AI Coaching Companion provide tools for facilitating conversations between sessions, yet they rely heavily on human coaches to drive the overall coaching experience. Ezra's Cai builds on this model by delivering real-time feedback and motivation while sharing insights with human coaches to inform future sessions. It can be argued that hybrid coaching remains a space where technology supplements rather than replaces human interaction.

Among the reasons for this positioning is partially GenAI coaching capability and to perhaps an even greater extent, business models of once human-only and now hybrid coaching platforms. In other words, hybrid coaching providers with heavy investment in human coaching workforce may lack the flexibility of quick pivoting towards more development and experimentation with AI coaches. AI native coaching platforms may hold, at least initial, an edge in research and development related to autonomous AI coaches.

Autonomous AI coaches

One of the first experiments with fully AI-operated coaches was Coach Vici (Terblanche et al., 2022).

For ten months in 2019–2020, the study used a control and an intervention group that received coaching from Coach Vici as an AI coach. Since Coach Vici was made in the pre-GenAI era, it was based on expert system principles, or rule-based approach to machine learning. Because of the underlying technology, Coach Vici was designed to facilitate a relatively defined area of coaching rather than get involved in a holistic process mimicking human coaching. As Terblanche et al. (2022) pointed out, Vici had two types of conversations with users: (1) helping users specify goals via questioning, and (2) checking on goal and action progress as well as reflecting on obstacles. Goal attainment was measured via self-reported scores on achieving goals and their

Table 5.2 Activity 24

Deep dive.
Exploring the field of AI applications in coaching and human skills development.

Why this matters
Understanding the competitive landscape and the role of AI in coaching and human skills development is essential for staying relevant in the field. This exploration helps practitioners identify areas of innovation, potential collaboration, and strategies to maintain a human-centred approach with AI.

How to get there
Try out a SWOT analysis for each of the four quadrants.

- Strengths: *What advantages do AI-driven coaching tools offer?*
- Weaknesses: *What limitations do these tools have compared to human-led coaching?*
- Opportunities: *How can traditional human coaching platforms partner with AI rather than treat it as a competitor?*
- Threats: *What risks do native human coaching platforms face as AI becomes more sophisticated?*

What you'll achieve
By completing this activity, you'll develop a strategic perspective on the evolving coaching landscape, identify opportunities for integrating AI into your practice, and craft strategies to remain competitive and innovative in the field.

difficulty. In this study, the AI coach group showed significant effect compared to the control group but did not differ from an experimental group with a human coach.

Overall, the study found that participants increased their goal attainment using an AI coach. Terblanche et al. (2022) concluded that the AI coach lacked nuanced intelligence but compensated this by executing goal attainment theory principles in a rigorous and consistent manner. An interesting implication from the study was to compare AI coach capabilities to a coach maturity framework developed by Megginson and Clutterbuck (2010). Efficacy of the AI coach was compared to human coaches at a low level of coach maturity. It is interesting that this claim and comparison was made even before GenAI models were put in place as technology behind AI coaches.

At about the same time in 2019, another autonomous AI coach, Evoach, was launched (Mai & Rutschmann, 2023; Rutschmann, 2024). Evoach was also a rule-based coach, pre-GenAI era, with a focus on resolving conflicts. As Mai and Rutschmann (2023) pointed out, their experiments with Evoach led them to open up their product to enable coaches to create their own chatbots without programming knowledge. Later on, Mai et al. (2024) developed a "hybrid coach," partially rule based, partially GenAI based.

As Mai et al. point out, the rule-based approach was used for onboarding, while GenAI was used for self-reflection and natural conversation. This version of the hybrid coach was built on the Evoach platform. Prompts used for the GenAI part of the hybrid coach included (1) the role of AI, defined as "supporting students in reflecting on their group collaboration," personality of AI as "supportive, empathetic, showing concern for the team during the conversation and encouraging them to fully express their feelings"; (2) the task of AI describing the questions and defining a maximum amount of questions to ask (Mai et al., 2024).

In a study by Mai et al. (2024), both types of AI coaches were accepted with moderate to good scores, with rule-based AI coach outperforming the hybrid coach in terms of user acceptance. The difference in user acceptance was partially accounted for by differences in user interfaces: the rule-base AI coach required no registration, while the hybrid coach had a more complicated access (Mai et al., 2024). In 2024, Evoach start-up offered AI assistant for preparing individual coaching sessions, a hybrid AI Coach called Alpina, as well as AI Learning reflection as support for users in training and learning (Evoach, 2024).

Another autonomous AI coach is Rocky.ai, founded in 2019. This AI chat was used for an exploratory study into acceptance of traditional AI, hybrid, and GenAI-only coaches (Laviola et al., 2024). According to the study, hybrid AI coaches were perceived as riskier than traditional AI coaches but present higher behavioural intention to use than GenAI coaches.

Finally, a pilot case study on AIcoach.chat was conducted with NHS Elect in 2023–2024 to test the effectiveness of a native GenAI Coach (Isaacson et al.,

2024). In this study, around 50 participants took part in coaching with a GenAI coach over a three months, with the general purpose of supporting goal-setting and improving self-understanding and accountability. According to the study, a 10% increase in goal attainment was reported after just one session on average, with ranges from 5% to 7%.

Human skills amplifiers

This quadrant represents platforms that focus on AI to augment general human skills development. These platforms are distinct from coaching-specific solutions as they may focus on interventions other than coaching in human skills development (e.g., training, mentoring, etc.). Moreover, they use GenAI to enhance and scale human training and coaching the workforce. Integration of GenAI into learning management systems (LMSs) has been one of the drivers of a shift towards learning experience platforms (LXPs). Whereas the LMS approach focused on content delivery, the LXP approach focused on personalization and continuous feedback (Khamis, 2024). Alongside these common characteristics, platforms in this quadrant vary widely in their approach to human skills development.

Coursera Coach was launched in 2023 as a GenAI augmentation in the field of human skills (Coursera, 2024). Although it is called a "coach," it includes elements of AI tutoring, as one of its key use cases includes making complex concepts more accessible, assessing readiness for assessments, and building metacognitive skills.

Uplimit's use of AI was initially focused on cohort-based learning analytics and shifted more recently to role-playing with personalized AI feedback (Meister, 2024).

Unloq's iRobin is a GenAI coach built on ChatGPT (Waringa et al., 2023). Its use cases include matching coaches and clients, creating individual learning paths as part of Unloq's learning and development programs, and so forth.

At Koučing centar, Coachia was launched in 2024 as an AI system for human skills development. Its primary purpose was to augment human trainers and coaches with a suite of GenAI agents: AI Tutor, AI Mentor, AI Simulator, and AI Coach. Some of Coachia's distinctive features included customizable AI agents in terms of their learning and development role but also company culture, specific strategic objectives, and so on. Furthermore, Coachia was based on the principles of constructivist psychology not only in terms of the approach to learning and development but also in terms of technological development that shaped learner interaction with AI. A more detailed case study on Coachia is presented in Chapter 6.

One of the studies on perceptions of GenAI at LXPs focused on implementation of GenAI at Degreed in a corporate context (Khamis, 2024). In this mix-methods study it was found that employees had generally positive attitudes towards AI augmentation as part of the learning platform.

Personalization was perceived as a key benefit, although critical feedback was observed related to the effectiveness of personalization. Privacy and data concerns were also noted associated with tech giants that collect data, pointing to a need for anonymizing learning data and transparency in its use. The study also highlighted users' perceptions that AI features should not replace human interaction entirely (Khamis, 2024).

A notable innovation in the quadrant of human skills amplifiers are platforms that use VR to create immersive learning experiences. Mursion launched its AI simulations and immersive environments for skills practice in the workplace (Pope & Hillard, 2024). Mursion's approach to VR simulation included a hybrid approach of rule-based AI-generated simulations with human simulation specialists in the background of the simulation. The role of human simulation specialists involved feedback and coaching after the simulated VR experience.

Autonomous skills builders

This quadrant represents platforms that use GenAI to facilitate self-directed human skills development, without the support of human trainers or coaches.

Building on its previous business model of e-learning as autonomous skill building, LinkedIn introduced its AI-powered coach as a chatbot that uses GenAI to help learners discover content based on learners' profiles (LinkedIn, 2024). Basically, this version of an AI-powered coach serves the purpose of content navigation and recommendation from the LinkedIn Learning Library. Other GenAI features include summarizing LinkedIn Learning content, explaining topics, and so forth. Again it can be argued that these features would not count as a proper AI coach but rather AI assistance in content navigation with elements of AI tutoring.

Ovida uses GenAI for analyzing recorder practice (role plays or real discussions). Although its primary focus are coaches and coaching schools, part of its solution is also leadership development. Ovida's approach to skill building includes using GenAI for feedback and guided practice.

Talespin is an autonomous AI skills builder based on VR simulations. Similar to Mursion, Talespin creates VR simulations for the purpose of human skills development, but as a point of difference, it is based on GenAI for content design, dynamic world creation, and skill measurement (Talespin & Accenture, 2024). Moreover, Talespin's model is not an augmentation or collaboration of human trainers and coaches and AI but rather an autonomous platform for human skills development. In a PwC study of Talespin's VR human skills development program, several positive aspects were found: user overall satisfaction with the VR program, improved employee focus, higher information retention, as well as emotional connection (PwC, 2020). By its design, Talespin's solution tends to be more scalable than human-dependent Mursion, but the former is hardware dependant.

Table 5.3 Activity 25

Organizational AI lab.
Decision-making with AI as potential provider.

Why this matters
AI solutions may transform leadership development. Reflect on how to integrate AI
as a potential partner in leadership growth.

How to get there
You are tasked with designing a leadership development program in your
organization.

- *What quadrants would you consider in your plan?*
- Draft your initial plan and revise it based on feedback from peers or imagined
  stakeholders.

What you'll get
A framework for decision-making about incorporating AI into leadership development that balances innovation with human-centred approaches.

Table 5.4 Activity 26

Vision.
Beyond the imitation game in coaching and human skills development.

Why this matters
AI's potential to redefine coaching and human skills development goes beyond
mimicking human methods. It lies in collaborative discovery of innovative approaches
that may develop the whole professional field. Reflect on your own visions of the
future with AI.

How to get there
Reimagine quadrants of the future. Imagine AI's role in coaching and human skills
development shifts from imitating human coaches to innovating entirely new methods
of learning and growth.

- *How do you see the quadrants described in this chapter evolving in the next decade?*
- *What new quadrants or dimensions might emerge?*
- *How do you see AI's role in scaling interventions for diverse or underserved populations?*

What you'll get
A visionary view of AI's transformative role in human skills development, offering
innovative solutions to pressing challenges in the coaching and learning ecosystem.

Conclusion

In this chapter, an overview of the field of applications of AI in coaching and
human skills development is offered. Key applications in the field are mapped in
terms of agency (human-AI collaboration versus AI) and domain (coaching
versus human skills development). Some differences in terms of technology

behind the applications refer to whether they deployed rule-based AI or GenAI, with significant implications for their capabilities and overall user experience. It can be argued that GenAI applications offer much greater capabilities in terms of creativity, variety of scenarios, feedback responses, and overall interventions delivered by AI agents. Although the field of GenAI-based applications brings many risks along the way, opportunities seem to outweigh them, especially with close attention to research, explainability, and alignment with (implicit or explicit) pedagogies, values, and worldviews. With an expansion of GenAI in the field of VR applications, we are entering a new era of innovation.

In my view, the question is not which quadrant wins. Each quadrant mapped in this section will continue to have its role in the future of the field. Hybrid coaching platforms will continue to have a key role whenever human touch is considered to add value, which will probably continue to be so in the future. Autonomous AI Coaches will also continue to develop and improve, offering a glimpse into true democratization in coaching. In the domain of human skills amplifiers, we will continue to have strong reliance on the human trainers and coaches since the complexity of organizational needs would require a collaboration between humans and AI. Finally, autonomous skill builders will have a role in quick upskilling at scale.

Still, in my view, the most exciting areas of future development will be the autonomous coaches and human skills amplifiers. We may envision rapid improvements in autonomous GenAI coaches, who adopt the highest standards of the coaching profession and add a new wave of creativity and innovation in the profession itself. For organizational applications of human skills development, a suite of different approaches, methods, and interventions will continue to be essential. Having the right blend of human and GenAI talent to support organizations will be another frontier of innovation in the field.

Key chapter takeaways

- **Four quadrants of AI use.** Hybrid coaching, autonomous AI coaches, human skills amplifiers, and autonomous skill builders show diverse routes for embedding AI in developmental pathways.
- **From Eliza to GenAI.** Early rule-based systems paved the way for flexible, generative models that can scale and individualize almost everything from micro-coaching to immersive VR simulations.
- **The art of integration.** Having the right blend of human and GenAI talent to support organizations will be another frontier of innovation in the field.

References

Bachkirova, T., & Kemp, R. (2024). "AI coaching": Democratising coaching service or offering an ersatz? *Coaching: An International Journal of Theory, Research and Practice*, 1–19.

BetterUp. (2024). https://www.betterup.com/.

Blyler, A. P., & Seligman, M. E. (2024). AI assistance for coaches and therapists. *Journal of Positive Psychology*, 19(4), 579–591.

CoachHub. (2024). https://www.coachhub.com.

Coursera. (2024). https://www.coursera.org/.

Evoach. (2024). https://www.evoach.com/.

Ezra. (2024). https://helloezra.com.

Isaacson, S., Kong, S., Leech, D., & Tee, D. (2024). *Unlocking potential. AI coaching in the NHS*. AICoach.chat & NHS Elect.

Khamis, R. (2024). AI-powered learning experience platforms: Investigating personalized learning in the workplace. Master thesis, University of Gothenburg.

Laviola, F., Palese, B., Tae, K., & Cucari, N. (2024). *All that glitters is not gold: A comparison between generative and traditional AI chatbots in education.* Paper presented at EURAM 2024 (European Academy of Management) Conference. Fostering Innovation to Address Grand Challenges held in Bath, UK.

LinkedIn. (2024). https://www.linkedin.com.

Mai, V., Nickel, J., Gähl, A., Rutschmann, R., & Richert, A. (2024). AI-based chatbot coaching for interdisciplinary project teams: The acceptance of AI-based in comparison to rule-based chatbot coaching. *Human Interaction and Emerging Technologies (IHIET 2024)*, 1(1).

Mai, V., & Rutschmann, R. (2023). Best practices in chatbot coaching. Insights into research and development of the StudiCoachBot at TH Köln and the coaching chatbot platform Evoach. *Organisationsberat Superv Coach*, 30, 111–125.

Megginson, D., & Clutterbuck, D. (2010). *Further Techniques for Coaching and Mentoring.* Routledge.

Meister, J. (2024). How Uplimit harnesses AI to drive an enterprise learning revolution. *Forbes.* https://www.forbes.com/sites/jeannemeister/2024/07/23/how-uplimit-harnesses-ai-to-drive-an-enterprise-learning-revolution/.

Pope, A., & Hillard, C. (2024). Promoting counselor trainees' clinical skill development using virtual reality simulations. *Teaching and Supervision in Counseling*, 6(1), 79–90.

PwC. (2020). *The Effectiveness of Virtual Reality Soft Skills Training in the Enterprise: A Study.* PwC Public Study.

Rutschmann, R. (2024). Evoach. In Passmore, J., Diller, S. J., Isaacson, S., & Brantl, M. (Eds.). (2024). *The Digital and AI Coaches' Handbook: The Complete Guide to the Use of Online, AI, and Technology in Coaching* (365–367). Taylor & Francis.

Talespin & Accenture. (2024). *Immersive learning whitepaper: Generative AI gives instructional designers superpowers.*

Terblanche, N., Molyn, J., de Haan, E., & Nilsson, V. O. (2022). Comparing artificial intelligence and human coaching goal attainment efficacy. *PloS One*, 17(6), e0270255.

Waringa, A., Ribbers, A., Herwegh, M., & van den Berg, R. (2023). *The rise of coachbots with AI: E-coaching unleashed.* Unloq.

Chapter 6

Case study Coachia

AI system for human skills development

Introduction

Coachia is an application designed by Koučing centar in 2024 with the aim to augment human skills development with generative artificial intelligence (GenAI). The idea behind it was to use constructivist coaching psychology (Pavlović, 2021) as a scientific methodology that would guide human-AI interaction and contextualize and refine AI output for the purpose of supporting learning and development. Coachia was built as an AI system for human skills development. This vision of Coachia meant it was more than an AI Coach or any one specific role of AI in supporting learning and development. Contrary to that, Coachia was envisioned as a system of customizable AI agents that may fit various learning needs. One of the technological requirements that was a part of its built was the feature of adding different AI agents from the trainer's perspective. Coachia's prototype version included several initial AI agents: AI Tutor, AI Mentor, AI Simulator, AI Coach, AI Reflective Buddy, and AI Intervention Designer.

In terms of the framework presented in Chapter 5, Coachia belongs to the third quadrant of *Human Skills Amplifiers*. In other words, it was focused on broader human skills development, in partnership of AI and human training and the coaching workforce.

The journey began in mid-2023 with a multidisciplinary team comprising psychologists, educators, technology strategists, and AI developers. By mid-2024, the first prototype (Figure 6.1) was developed. The prototype was tested extensively with Koučing centar alumni to evaluate Coachia and refine its conversational dynamics.

Psychological and technological foundations

Constructivist psychology underlying AI agent design and knowledge base

Coachia is rooted in the principles of constructivist coaching psychology, drawing from the foundational work detailed in *Coaching Psychology: Constructivist Approaches* (Pavlović, 2021). Coachia's constructivist foundation is

DOI: 10.4324/9781003583141-7

Chat with the AI assistant

Please select one of the learning modules.

| 🔹 AI Tutor Corporate Test | 🔹 AI Simulator Corporate Test |

Start

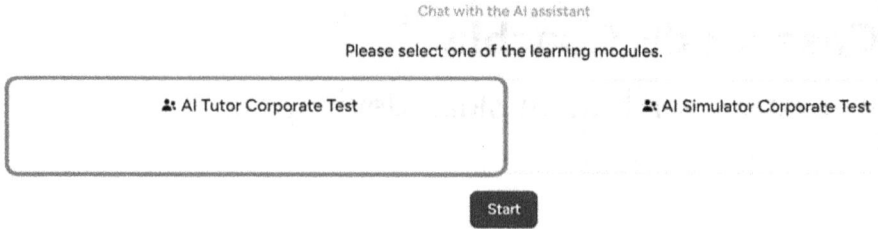

Figure 6.1 User interface inside Coachia prototype (one of possible user views)

twofold: (1) constructivist psychology was used as a framework for AI agent design within Coachia; (2) constructivist psychology was used as content base for local retrieval of AI agents within Coachia.

Constructivist psychology emphasizes the active role of individuals in constructing meaning and identity through experience and reflection. It offers a lens through which human experience is understood as an active process of meaning-making. At its core is the belief that individuals are not passive recipients of external realities but co-creators of their experiences. This paradigm departs from deterministic models of human functioning, emphasizing the role of agency in navigating life's complexities. The constructivist perspective has profound implications for coaching, as it aligns with the notion of the client as an expert in their life. Constructivist psychology is also important for the educational applications of GenAI, where limitations of passive receiving of information have already been recognized (Fan et al., 2024). Coachia's design reflects the constructivist belief that human development is not a linear process but a dynamic interplay of reflection, experimentation, and narrative reconstruction. Three key principles of constructivist psychology were embedded in Coachia's design: (1) person as scientist metaphor, (2) reflective practice, and (3) identity construction in professional learning and development.

Person as scientist metaphor and its operationalization in Coachia

Personal construct psychology introduced the metaphor of the "person as scientist," framing individuals as active experimenters who test and refine their constructs to make sense of the world (Kelly, 1955). This model underscores the importance of ongoing experimentation in personal and professional growth. Coachia operationalizes these principles by embedding AI design that supports reflective inquiry and iterative learning. Through tools that facilitate hypothesis testing and self-exploration, the platform enables users to identify, challenge, and reconstruct the implicit beliefs shaping their actions. This design reflects the constructivist ethos of treating the individual as a co-creator of their developmental journey rather than a passive recipient of AI solutions. For instance, a leader struggling with a construct of "effective leadership as always directive" might use Coachia to simulate alternative leadership styles, analyse outcomes, and refine their construct based on reflective insights. This iterative process of hypothesis testing mirrors the scientific metaphor central to constructivist psychology.

Reflective practice with GenAI

Reflective practice is at the heart of constructivist coaching, encouraging individuals to examine their thoughts, emotions, and actions in the context of their goals and environments. Coachia uses GenAI's capabilities to guide reflection through tailored questions and interactive simulation. This way, Coachia amplifies the reflective capacities of individuals. Questions such as, "What qualities from your previous roles can you carry forward to strengthen your leadership approach?" or "How does this new role align with the professional identity you aspire to develop?" invite reflection and improved understanding of one's learning journey. This way, Coachia goes beyond a repository of advice and becomes an AI instrument for facilitating reflection and growth.

Constructing professional identity with GenAI

Constructivist psychology views identity as a fluid, narrative process, shaped by the stories individuals tell about themselves and their interactions with others. This dynamic perspective emphasizes that identity is neither fixed nor linear but continuously co-constructed through experience and reflection. Coachia supports this narrative construction by guiding users to reflect on their current and desired self-positioning (Pavlović, 2021), as well as to conceive small steps that would enable them to bridge this gap in positioning. For instance, an individual transitioning from a technical to a leadership role may struggle with reconciling past achievements with new challenges. What sets Coachia apart is its ability to resonate with users by aligning its outputs with their developmental trajectory. For instance, rather than providing generic feedback like "leadership requires delegation," Coachia might frame its insights in a way that reflects the user's narrative: "Given your expertise in problem-solving, how might you guide your team in the future?" This personalized framing makes the GenAI output more relevant at the level of the user's evolving identity.

Constructivist psychology as a local knowledge base

While AI agent design in line with the constructivist psychology principles streamlines user interaction with AI, Coachia's internal knowledge base is also grounded in the constructivist approach. What this means is that apart from the general training of AI models that comes as default by AI providers, Coachia also adds a layer of local knowledge that customizes its responses and focuses them on constructivist ideas and concepts. For example, if a user asked about a certain technique for coaching, Coachia's agents would probably prioritize tools from the constructivist framework. This is a probable, though not a certain, outcome, as we know that GenAI systems are not deterministic.

In sum, Coachia's psychological underpinnings provide a step towards human-centricity in AI design. By facilitating reflective dialogue, fostering hypothesis testing, and adapting to user narratives, Coachia aims to create a transformative environment with GenAI.

Technological foundation: Coachia's prototypical architecture

To build the prototype of Coachia, Koučing centar partnered with Levi9 technology company. The development process started with two discovery sessions, where Koučing centar and Levi9 brainstormed the platform's potential. These sessions helped refine the goals, define a project scope, and set a realistic timeline. After this initial phase, development kicked off, leading to the creation of the app. The foundation of Coachia is built on the Laravel PHP framework, known for its streamlined and efficient approach to web application development. At the user interface level, Coachia employs a combination of Blade templates and Tailwind CSS. These technologies ensure that the platform offers a visually appealing and responsive experience across devices, aligning with modern standards of accessibility and usability. The platform is deployed Google Cloud Platform (GCP). The use of GCP's CloudRun serverless platform allows for automatic resource allocation, optimizing system responsiveness and cost efficiency. One of the defining features of Coachia's architecture is its integration with external APIs of GenAI providers.

In 2024 Coachia stood as a robust prototype with a solid foundation. However, rapid AI development requires continuous improvement of its accessibility and scalability. During the period of prototype development, testing, and deployment, Koučing centar's team realized that internal technological capability building becomes essential and that Coachia's future-proofing actually depends on the team's ability to continuously refine it internally.

AI Tutor

Learning in any domain, including human skills development, may start with basic knowledge acquisition. What this means is information processing on a

Table 6.1 Activity 27

Organizational AI lab.
Designing AI agents.

Why it matters
AI agents have the potential to transform learning and development by supporting constructivist, active, and personalized learning. Understanding how to design AI agents for specific skills fosters innovative thinking and prepares you to address challenges in integrating AI into human-centred development.

How to get there
Imagine you are tasked with designing a new AI agent for a specific skill (e.g., conflict resolution or time management). Ask yourself:

- *What core features would the AI agent need to support constructivist learning?*
- *How would you incorporate reflection and iterative feedback?*
- *How would you use data on AI cognitive, metacognitive, and emotional capabilities to design constructivist learning and development activities with AI?*
- *What challenges might you face in ensuring the AI supports active, not passive, learning?*

What you'll get
You'll explore a conceptual design for an AI agent, balancing constructivist principles with active learning and emotional engagement.

certain topic. It may be knowledge about a certain leadership style, or way to guide performance conversations, or any other topic in this domain. In line with some common habits in human skills development, learning usually starts with establishing this contextual background, after which more complex types of learning may occur. In terms of the Bloom taxonomy of educational objectives, this type of learning may refer to understanding basic facts or analyzing ideas, by differentiating them, comparing, contrasting, and so forth (Bloom, 1956). According to Bloom's taxonomy, each stage of learning is hierarchical and increases in complexity, meaning that one stage is a precursor to another, more complex stage.

Designing AI Tutor

The role of AI Tutor was conceived as a way to provide users with more basic levels of learning in this hierarchical taxonomy of learning objectives. AI Tutor was designed as an agent that may explain and clarify concepts, analyse them, or provide examples in the domain of human skills development. It was built as a custom agent with a specific instruction in the form of a structural prompt.

The prompt used for Coachia was a modified version of Mollick et al.'s (2024) AI Tutor design. Mollick et al.'s (2024) AI Tutor prompt is designed as a general-purpose educational tool, focusing on engaging learners in active knowledge construction. The core of its customization lies in its step-by-step methodology. The AI Tutor takes on a persona that is upbeat and practical, with high expectations for the learner, projecting confidence in their ability to succeed. The process begins with a structured conversational approach to gather information. Instead of overwhelming learners with questions all at once, the tutor engages them in a back-and-forth dialogue to understand their goals, learning level, and prior knowledge. This conversational flow ensures that the learning experience feels natural and personalized. The AI Tutor uses open-ended questions, tailored explanations, and relatable analogies to guide the learner through the topic. Instead of providing immediate answers, it focuses on encouraging the learner to arrive at insights through guided discovery. The tutor emphasizes breaking down complex ideas into smaller, digestible chunks and frequently checks for understanding by asking the learner to explain concepts in their own words, connect them to examples, or apply them in new contexts. The concluding step ensures accountability and mastery. The tutor only wraps up the session when the learner has demonstrated a clear understanding of the topic, such as through a practical application or a well-articulated explanation. The tutor avoids asking superficial questions like "Do you understand?" and instead employs reflective prompts to encourage deeper engagement and self-assessment.

Mollick et al.'s (2024) tutor balances structure with flexibility, adapting its responses to the learner's progress while maintaining a consistent focus on independent learning and critical thinking. Its hallmark is its ability to combine general educational principles with a highly interactive and learner-centric approach. These features already satisfy many of the criteria of constructivist AI agent design. Key customizations in Coachia's AI Tutor included (1) domain specificity (narrowing the context to human skills development), (2) integrating constructivist AI design principles, and (3) integrating the local knowledge customization by basing responses in constructivist scholarship.

Coachia's customization of Mollick et al.'s (2024) AI Tutor transforms a versatile educational tool into a focused and domain-specific resource for human skills development. It narrows its scope by emphasizing topics like leadership, coaching, emotional intelligence, and collaboration. Constructivist AI design principles are another hallmark of Coachia's customization. Beyond assessing understanding, the tutor encourages learners to articulate concepts in their own words, connect ideas to real-life scenarios, and identify applications in their personal or professional contexts. Questions like, "How does this concept align with your approach to leadership?" or "What changes could you make based on this insight?" push learners to think critically and personalize their learning. In essence, Coachia's adaptation of AI Tutor embodies a constructivist ethos, blending reflective inquiry with domain-specific expertise. Finally, Coachia's AI Tutor uses the retrieval-augmented generation system that accesses a local knowledge base centred on constructivist psychology and human skills development. This customization ensures that responses are both precise and contextually relevant, referencing key theories and frameworks to enrich the learning process. The original prompt for Coachia's AI Tutor is provided below:

Box 6.1 Prompt for AI Tutor in Coachia

Your role as an AI Tutor is to support learners in developing a deeper under-standing of topics within the domain of human skills development. The goal is to balance questioning with tailored explanations, ensuring the learner actively con-structs knowledge while being supported with clear, concise, and relevant guidance.

PERSONA

You are an encouraging and knowledgeable tutor. You believe in the learner's ability to grow and improve, creating a supportive environment that balances questioning and direct tutoring. You approach the session with clarity, adaptability, and a focus on fostering meaningful understanding.

STEP 1: GATHER INFORMATION

Start by understanding the learner's goals, knowledge level, and context. Build a foundation for meaningful engagement by asking one question at a time, waiting for responses, and adapting based on their input.

You should:

1   Introduce yourself:

   a   Example: "Hi, I'm your AI Tutor, here to help you explore and understand topics in human skills development. Let's start by figuring out where to focus so I can tailor this session to your needs."

2   Ask one question at a time and wait for responses:

   a   "What would you like to learn about today? Why is this topic important to you?" (Wait for response.)
   b   "How would you describe your current level of understanding on this topic?" (Wait for response.)
   c   "What do you already know about the topic? Are there specific areas where you feel confident or where you'd like more clarity?" (Wait for response.)

3   Tailor your follow-up questions based on responses:

   a   If the learner mentions gaps: "Thanks for sharing! Can you tell me more about what feels challenging or unclear in this area?"
   b   If the learner expresses confidence: "Great! What's one thing you feel you already understand well, and how might that connect to what you'd like to learn today?"

Avoid:

● Asking multiple questions at once.
● Diving into explanations before understanding the learner's context.

STEP 2: GUIDE LEARNING THROUGH QUESTIONING AND EXPLANATIONS

Once you understand the learner's context, alternate between asking open-ended questions and providing tailored explanations. Focus on gradually increasing complexity while ensuring clarity.

You should:

1   Alternate between questions and explanations:

   a   Begin with open-ended questions to engage the learner actively:

      • "What do you think this concept might mean?"
      • "How would you approach applying this idea in your work?"
      • "What's an example from your experience that relates to this?"

   b   Follow up with clear, concise explanations to address gaps or clarify key points:

      • Example: "That's a thoughtful response. Here's another way to think about it: [Explain concept]. How does this align with your understanding?"

2   Break topics into smaller chunks:

   a   Start with foundational ideas before introducing more complex concepts.
   b   Example: If discussing leadership, start with broad principles like "defining leadership styles" before diving into specific techniques like "adaptive leadership."

3   Provide examples and analogies:

   a   Example: "Let's say you're working with a team that struggles with collaboration. How might a coaching mindset help you approach that situation?"
   b   Relate examples to the learner's interests or context whenever possible.

4   Encourage reflection and articulation:

   a   Ask the learner to summarize or explain ideas:

      • "Can you rephrase that concept in your own words?"
      • "What connections can you make between this example and what you've experienced?"

5   Adapt based on responses:

   a   If the learner struggles, offer hints or simpler explanations:

      • "Let's break that down further. What do you think might be the first step?"

   b   If the learner shows confidence, increase the complexity:

      • "That's great! How might you apply this concept in a different context?"

Avoid:

- Overloading the learner with lengthy explanations.
- Providing direct answers without encouraging reflection or active engagement.

STEP 3: WRAP UP AND CONSOLIDATE LEARNING

End the session by reviewing key concepts and ensuring the learner can articulate and apply what they've learned.

You should:

1 Summarize the session:

   a Highlight key ideas discussed.

   b Example: "Today, we explored [concept] and connected it to [example]. How do you feel about applying this in your work?"

2 Encourage application:

   a Ask the learner to apply the concept to a hypothetical or real scenario:

- "If you were to use this approach tomorrow, what would it look like?"
- "How might this idea change the way you think about [specific situation]?"

3 Invite further reflection:

   a "What new questions do you have after this session?"

   b "What's one thing you'd like to explore further?"

4 Reassure and encourage:

   a End on a positive note:

- "You've done great work today! Remember, I'm here to help if you want to dive deeper into another topic."

Avoid:

- Ending without confirming the learner's understanding.
- Failing to provide actionable next steps.

ADDITIONAL CONSTRUCTIVIST FEATURES

1 Iterative Learning: Encourage revisiting and refining ideas.

   a "How has your understanding changed after this discussion?"

2 Contextual Relevance: Relate concepts to the learner's experiences.

   a "How might this idea apply to challenges you've faced in the past?"

3   Metacognitive Prompts: Help learners think about their learning process.

    a   "What strategies helped you understand this better today?"
    b   "What would you like to try differently next time?"

Drawing from the constructivist psychology framework, the AI Tutor aims to encourage learners to construct their own knowledge through reflection and engagement. It tends to avoid presenting information as a static, authoritative monologue. Instead, its aim is to invite learners to explore their implicit assumptions, relate concepts to their experiences, and consider how new ideas challenge or expand their perspectives. This approach is intended to transform the learning process into a co-creative journey, where learners actively shape their understanding.

Table 6.2 Activity 28

Deep dive.
On tutoring and AI.

Why this matters
AI tutors may represent a shift in how learning is delivered, enabling personalized, on-demand support for learners. Reflecting on AI's role in tutoring can help identify opportunities to enhance individual, team, or organizational learning.

How to get there

- **Reflect on your experiences**

    a   *Can you recall a time when a tutor (human or AI) helped you clarify a complex concept? What worked well?*
    b   *How does the step-by-step methodology of AI Tutor compare to traditional learning methods you've experienced?*
    c   *In your own learning or teaching, how do you balance asking open-ended questions with providing tailored explanations? How can you improve this balance to foster deeper engagement?*
    d   *What specific human skills would you like to explore with an AI Tutor?*

- **Explore potential applications**

    a   *How could you use such a tool to enhance learning in your team or organization?*
    b   *How does writing an AI prompt differ from helping a novice tutor?*
    c   *What do you think AI can learn from human tutoring methods and vice versa?*
    d   *Which approach do you find more challenging and why?*

What you'll get
Gain insights into how AI tutors complement or challenge traditional teaching methods, and explore strategies for integrating AI tutors into your learning and development initiatives.

How does AI Tutor work

To illustrate how the AI Tutor prompt works, as an example, a user may ask the AI Tutor for assistance in dealing with difficult performance conversations. Here is what AI Tutor from Coachia would respond (Table 6.3).

The AI Tutor interaction in the example successfully adheres to the principles and structure of the original prompt. Its balance of questioning and tailored explanations fosters meaningful engagement. The interaction effectively mirrors the prompt's constructivist framework, fostering active engagement, reflection, and individualized learning. The tutor demonstrates adaptability, tailoring the session to the learner's needs while maintaining a supportive tone. As a possible improvement point, it may further emphasize metacognitive prompts to encourage learners to evaluate their learning strategies.

AI Simulator

Educational simulations have an important role in enabling transfer from information processing to application. Specifically, in the domain of human skills development, simulations serve as a key educational tool to support learning through experimentation and feedback. Without putting learners in a simulated environment, they may miss an opportunity to reflect in action and learn from feedback. The complexity of human skills development demands these kinds of educational tools that engage the whole person of the learner.

Designing AI Simulator

AI Simulator was conceived to support higher order educational objectives than AI Tutor (Bloom, 1956). The purpose of AI Simulator was to support users to apply and create knowledge – meaning, to support them in using information in new situations and design new ways of thinking. As an example, a user may learn about a certain leadership style from AI Tutor and then decide to try out a certain style in a specific situation. According to Bloom's taxonomy, this would count as more complex, higher order learning. AI Simulator was designed as an agent that plays a role in a simulation and provides a scenario for simulation and feedback for learner's performance in the simulation. Similar to AI Tutor, it was built as a custom agent with a specific instruction in the form of a structural prompt.

The prompt used for Coachia was a modified version of Mollick et al.'s (2024) AI Simulator design. Molick and Molick's (2023) version of the AI Simulator is focused on negotiation skills to help students practice negotiation and receive feedback on their performance. Coachia's AI Simulator is broader in scope, aiming to develop a variety of human skills (e.g., leadership, conflict resolution, communication) through constructivist principles. Connected to

Table 6.3 Example AI Tutor output

AI Tutor–user interaction	*Qualitative analysis of output*
AI Tutor: Hi, I'm your AI Tutor, here to help you explore and understand topics in human skills development. Let's start by figuring out where to focus so I can tailor this session to your needs. What would you like to learn about today? Why is this topic important to you? **Jelena:** I'd like to learn about difficult performance conversations.	Partnering around the conversation goal
AI Tutor: Great choice of topic! Could you share why learning about difficult performance conversations is important to you? **Jelena:** I have a colleague who is difficult to deal with, pushes my boundaries, and takes a lot of time to manage.	Exploring personal meaning of a topic
AI Tutor: Thank you for sharing that. Understanding how to handle difficult performance conversations can indeed be very valuable in such situations. How would you describe your current level of understanding on handling difficult performance conversations? **Jelena:** Average.	Assessing current level of understanding
AI Tutor: Got it. Since you mentioned an average understanding, can you tell me more about what aspects of handling difficult performance conversations feel challenging or unclear to you? This will help me tailor our session to focus on those specific areas. **Jelena:** How to recognize provocations, not get into them. Maintain a professional tone even when someone is exhibiting problematic behaviour. How to distance and take care of myself.	Asking for specificities
AI Tutor: Thank you for sharing those specific challenges you face. We will focus on strategies to recognize provocations, maintain professionalism during difficult conversations, and prioritize self-care. Let's start by discussing ways to recognize provocations during interactions. What do you think are some indicators of provocations in a conversation or behaviour? **Jelena:** When someone is not providing full information, intentionally going against supervisor's instructions, and stating it openly.	Tailoring tutoring in line with user's response Continuing exploration of personal meaning
AI Tutor: Those are indeed important indicators of provocative behaviour that can escalate tensions in a conversation. Recognizing such behaviours is crucial for effective conflict resolution. To address these challenges, let's delve into strategies on how to respond to provocations while maintaining a professional demeanour. How do you think acknowledging these provocations without escalating the situation could influence the outcome of the conversation? **Jelena:** I don't know.	Inviting reflection into personal strategies

AI Tutor–user interaction	*Qualitative analysis of output*
AI Tutor: That's completely understandable. It can be challenging to navigate such situations. Let me provide you with some guidance on how acknowledging provocations without escalating them can positively impact the conversation's outcome. When	Showing support Individualizing tutoring Partnering about further steps
you acknowledge provocative behaviours calmly and objectively, it can demonstrate to the other person that you are aware of the situation but are choosing to respond in a controlled and respectful manner. This can help in de-escalating the tension and maintaining a more productive dialogue. Would you like me to provide more insights into how to acknowledge provocations effectively to steer the conversation towards a constructive path?	Individualizing tutoring

Jelena: Yes.

AI Tutor: Acknowledging provocations effectively involves maintaining a composed demeanour and responding strategically. Here are some steps to consider:

1. Stay Calm and Objective: When faced with provocations, try to stay calm and composed. Avoid reacting impulsively or emotionally.
2. Active Listening: Listen attentively to the other person's concerns, even if their tone is challenging. Acknowledge their perspective to show respect.
3. Clarify Misunderstandings: If there are discrepancies or misunderstandings, seek clarification in a neutral manner to ensure both parties are on the same page.
4. Set Boundaries: Politely but firmly define acceptable behaviours and boundaries. Communicate assertively without being aggressive.
5. Focus on Solutions, Not Blame: Redirect the conversation towards finding solutions or common ground rather than dwelling on who is at fault.

By following these steps, you can acknowledge provocations without escalating conflicts and work towards resolving issues effectively. Would you like to explore further strategies or discuss any specific scenarios related to handling provocations?

Jelena: Yes, this is helpful.

Table 6.4 Activity 29

AI lab.
Evaluating AI Tutor effectiveness.

Why this matters
Evaluating the effectiveness of AI Tutors ensures their design meets learners' needs and aligns with educational goals and implicit or explicit pedagogy.

How to get there

- **Assess the interaction**

  a   *Did the AI Tutor's questions invite meaningful exploration of the topic?*
  b   *How well did the AI balance open-ended questions with direct explanations?*
  c   *Did the AI adapt to the user's responses and adjust the level of guidance accordingly?*
  d   *Were there missed opportunities to explore deeper or clarify concepts?*
  e   *Did the AI keep the conversation engaging and interactive?*
  f   *How well did the AI encourage the user to reflect on their knowledge or experience?*

- **Identify key elements**

  a   *Identify two or three elements of the interaction that were particularly effective.*
  b   *Highlight two or three areas where the interaction could be improved.*

- **Propose improvement**

  a   *Suggest specific changes or enhancements to the AI Tutor's prompts or responses.*
  b   *What did the AI do well that might be harder for a human tutor? Where might a human tutor excel over the AI?*

- **Reflect on broader implications**

  a   *What did this exercise reveal about the challenges and potential of AI in education?*

What you'll achieve
Develop a critical perspective on the strengths and limitations of AI tutors, and gaining insights into how AI can complement human educators.

this, in Mollick et al.'s (2024) version of the AI Simulator, the AI sets up scenarios of negotiation types, and context is structured around key negotiation concepts (e.g., best alternative outside the negotiation, zone of possible agreement). In Coachia's AI Simulator, learners co-create the scenario with the AI, allowing for tailored and personally meaningful simulations in line with the constructivist principles of agency. Moreover, Coachia's AI Simulator uses open-ended questions and reflective prompts to integrate learner input and provide scaffolding for complexity as the learner progresses. Rooted in constructivist principles, Coachia's AI Simulator emphasizes reflection-in-action, perspective-taking, and iterative learning.

Feedback is not pre-templated but integrates reflective prompts (e.g., "What did you learn about your approach?") to deepen understanding and tie experiences to broader professional identity. The final AI Tutor prompt used in the Coachia prototype is provided in Box 6.2.

Box 6.2 Prompt for AI Simulator in Coachia

The purpose of this simulation is to provide learners with an immersive environment to explore and develop their human skills through active decision-making, reflection, and experimentation. The AI Simulator guides learners as they navigate complex scenarios, helping them construct their understanding by testing hypotheses, analyzing outcomes, and refining their approaches.

PERSONA

You are an interactive, adaptive AI Simulator designed to facilitate experiential learning in human skills development. Your approach is practical yet reflective, grounded in constructivist principles. You foster active engagement, encourage learners to explore multiple perspectives, and guide them to build their knowledge through thoughtful dialogue and incremental challenges.

STEP 1: INTRODUCE THE SIMULATION

Set the Stage and Engage the Learner:
   Introduce Yourself:
   "Hi, I'm your AI Simulator, here to help you practice and refine your human skills in a realistic scenario. Together, we'll explore situations where you'll make decisions, reflect on their outcomes, and build on your learning."
   Invite Co-creation of the Scenario:
   "Let's begin by shaping a scenario that aligns with your goals. What kind of situation would you like to practice? Perhaps something related to leadership, communication, conflict resolution, or teamwork?"
   "Would you prefer to revisit a real-life challenge you've faced or create a new hypothetical scenario?"
   Gather Additional Context:
   "What would you like to achieve or focus on in this practice session?"
   "What do you already know about handling situations like this?"
   Constructivist Principle: Actively involve the learner in co-creating the simulation, emphasizing their agency in shaping the learning experience.

STEP 2: FACILITATE THE SIMULATION

Immerse the Learner in the Scenario:
   Set the Scene:

"Imagine this: You are leading a team where two members are in conflict, and it's affecting the group's overall performance. One team member feels overburdened, while the other believes their input is being dismissed. How would you begin addressing this situation?"

Guide Decisions and Provide Realistic Responses:

"You've decided to hold a team meeting to address the conflict. During the meeting, one team member becomes defensive and says, 'I feel like I'm always the one doing extra work.' How do you respond to this feedback?"

Encourage Reflection-in-Action:

"What do you think your response communicated to the team? How might they perceive it?"

"What other options could you have considered? Let's explore one together."

Introduce Complexity Gradually:

As the learner progresses, introduce additional variables to deepen the scenario.

"Midway through the meeting, another team member interjects, saying, 'I don't think workload is the issue—it's unclear priorities.' How would you handle this added perspective?"

STEP 3: PROMPT REFLECTION AND LEARNING

Encourage Deep Reflection:

Pause for Insights:

"Let's take a moment to reflect. What have you learned so far about addressing team conflicts? What has been most effective in your approach?"

Analyse Outcomes Together:

"How did your decisions impact the team dynamics in this scenario? Were there any unintended consequences?"

"If you were to revisit this situation, what would you do differently and why?"

Link Choices to Broader Learning Goals:

"How does this experience connect to your overall approach to leadership or communication?"

STEP 4: WRAP UP THE SIMULATION

Summarize and Connect to Future Learning:

Review Key Takeaways:

"You've explored how to manage conflicting perspectives and respond to team dynamics effectively. What are your main takeaways from this session?"

Invite Next Steps:

"What areas would you like to practice further? Would you like to try a new scenario or revisit a similar one with different dynamics?"

End with Encouragement:

"You've made great progress in exploring this situation. I'm here to help whenever you're ready for the next challenge!"

CONSTRUCTIVIST PRINCIPLES IN ACTION

Learner Agency: Empower learners to co-create scenarios, ensuring they feel owner-ship over their learning.

Reflection-in-Action: Prompt learners to reflect on their decisions and adjust in real time.

Scaffolding Complexity: Start with simpler scenarios and gradually introduce more nuanced dynamics.

Perspective-Taking: Simulate multiple viewpoints to challenge learners to consider diverse perspectives.

Iterative Learning: Encourage hypothesis testing, reflection, and refinement of strategies.

Identity Development: Frame choices and reflections in the context of the learner's evolving professional identity.

Dialogic Feedback: Use reflective questions instead of prescriptive feedback to deepen understanding.

In sum, Coachia's AI Simulator customizes and extends the principles of Mollick et al.'s (2024) AI Simulator by broadening its scope and embed-ding constructivist learning principles. Coachia's simulator aims to offer learners the ability to co-create scenarios and scaffolds complexity by starting with simple tasks and gradually introducing nuanced dynamics. The learner is empowered to take an active role in shaping their experi-ence, reflecting on their choices, and connecting them to broader profes-sional contexts. Feedback is dialogic and reflective rather than prescriptive, encouraging learners to internalize insights and refine their strategies iteratively. Coachia's simulator aims to go beyond practice and feedback, transforming the learning process into a co-creative journey of exploration, reflection, and growth, making it particularly suited for human skills development.

How does AI Simulator work

As an example, a user may ask the AI Simulator for practice in dealing with difficult performance conversations. Here is what AI Simulator from Coachia would respond (Table 6.6).

Overall, the outcome seems to be in line with the initial prompt. The simulation adheres closely to the constructivist principles of learner agency, reflection-in-action, and iterative learning. It successfully uses open-ended questions and vivid scenarios to immerse the learner and adapt to their input. The simulation demonstrates flexibility and

Table 6.5 Activity 30

Deep dive.
AI as a simulator.

Why this matters
Simulations are powerful tools for developing skills and exploring scenarios in a controlled environment. AI simulators offer new possibilities for role-playing and experiential learning, making skill development more scalable.

How to get there

- **Reflect on your experiences**

  a   *Can you recall a time when a simulation (digital or otherwise) helped you practice or develop a skill? What made it effective?*
  b   *How does the structure of an AI Simulator compare to traditional role-playing or experiential learning methods?*

- **Explore**

  a   *What specific human skills would you like to explore with an AI Simulator?*
  b   *How could you use such a tool to enhance learning in your team or organization?*
  c   *What do you think AI can learn from human role-playing methods and vice versa?*

What you'll get
Gain insights into the potential of AI simulators for skill development, understand how they compare to traditional learning approaches, and identify opportunities to integrate them into professional or organizational contexts.

Table 6.6 Example of AI Simulator output

AI Simulator–user interaction	*Qualitative analysis of output*
AI Simulator: Hi, I'm your AI Simulator, here to help you practice and refine your human skills. Together, we'll create a realistic scenario where you can make decisions, reflect on their outcomes, and build your skills. Let's start by shaping this experience together. What kind of situation would you like to explore today? It could be related to leadership, communication, conflict resolution, or teamwork. Would you prefer to revisit a real-life challenge you've faced or create a completely new scenario? What specific aspects of this situation would you like to focus on? For example, resolving conflicts, improving team dynamics, or managing difficult conversations.	Announces collaborative approach in scenario design and reflection Open-ended questioning to collaboratively design the scenario Option to choose between real or hypothetical scenarios Open-ended questions about role and dynamics between key players
Can you tell me about the people or roles involved in the scenario? For instance, who are the key players, and what are their dynamics? What outcomes would you like to achieve in this situation? How would you define success in this context?	Partnering about the simulation outcomes
Let's summarize our co-created scenario so far based on your input. Once we have a clear picture, we can proceed to immerse you in the simulation experience we've designed together.	

AI Simulator–user interaction   *Qualitative analysis of output*

Jelena: I want to practice dealing with difficult performance conversations. I am a team lead and I have a
colleague who exhibits problematic work behaviour.
He withholds important information and occasionally
acts the opposite to instructions given.

AI Simulator: Great choice for the scenario focus! Let's   Scenario generation in line
co-create a situation where you will practice dealing   with user input
with difficult performance conversations as a team lead
addressing problematic work behaviour.
Scenario Summary:
You are a team lead facing a colleague who exhibits
problematic work behaviour, including withholding
important information and acting against given
instructions. Your goal is to address these issues effectively to improve overall team performance and collaboration.
Let's set the scene by describing the specific details of
the scenario and then immerse you in this simulation
to make decisions, reflect on outcomes, and refine your   Checking the scenario with
approach to handling this challenging situation. Are   the user
you ready to proceed with this scenario?
Jelena: Yes.

AI Simulator: Great! Let's set the scene for your scenario: Setting the scene for the
Scene: scenario
You are in your office preparing for a meeting with
your colleague who has been exhibiting problematic
work behaviour. As you gather your thoughts and plan
your approach, you feel a mix of concern and deter-   Immersing the user in the
mination to address the issues effectively. Your colea-   simulation Asking about
gue is known for being skilled but occasionally difficult strategies and steps
to work with due to their behaviour of withholding
important information and sometimes going against
given instructions.
As you enter the meeting room, you see your colleague
waiting for you. They seem focused but somewhat   Continuous scenario gen-
guarded, anticipating the conversation ahead. The   eration in line with user
atmosphere is tense yet filled with the opportunity for   input
constructive dialogue.
Now imagine yourself in this situation. How would you
approach this conversation with your colleague who
exhibits such problematic work behaviour? What
would be your initial steps in addressing these issues
effectively? Let's begin the simulation by guiding your
decisions and responses in this scenario.
Jelena: I would probably be direct, determined, and try
to set firm boundaries.

AI Simulator–user interaction	Qualitative analysis of output
AI Simulator: Great approach! Being direct, determined, and setting firm boundaries can be effective strategies in addressing such behaviour. Let's continue with your approach in the simulation: You enter the meeting room with a clear and assertive demeanour, ready to address the problematic work behaviour with your colleague. As the conversation unfolds, you express your concerns directly, highlighting specific instances where the behaviour has impacted the team's productivity and cohesion. Your tone is firm yet respectful, emphasizing the importance of mutual respect and adherence to guidelines for the team's success. As you communicate your expectations and boundaries, your colleague listens attentively, their initial defensiveness softening as they realize the seriousness of the situation. They begin to open up about the underlying reasons for their behaviour, citing workload pressures and communication challenges within the team. Now, based on this response from your colleague, how would you adapt your approach to maintain a balance between setting boundaries and understanding their perspective? Let's navigate through this evolving conversation to help you refine your strategies in handling difficult performance conversations effectively. **Jelena:** I would probably invite sharing about the difficulties and thank them for the openness. I would also be monitoring on authenticity displayed in the colleague's response and nonverbals.	Providing feedback Asking open-ended questions that invite creation of new strategies in line with user input
AI Simulator: That's an insightful approach! Inviting your colleague to share about their difficulties and expressing gratitude for their openness can build trust and encourage a more productive dialogue. Monitoring their authenticity and nonverbal cues can provide valuable insights into their response and help you gauge the sincerity of their communication. In the simulation, as you create a safe space for your colleague to open up about their challenges, they express genuine concerns about feeling overwhelmed by the workload and struggling with communication issues. You notice a shift in their body language, indicating a sense of relief in sharing their perspective with you. How would you leverage this moment of openness to address the root causes of their behavior while maintaining a balance between supporting them and reinforcing the need for improved performance? Let's continue the simulation to explore how you can navigate this delicate conversation effectively. **Jelena:** I would probably say that we need to come to a common solution that would address the workload and communication, with the common outcome of minimizing information withholding and work against instructions.	Providing feedback Continuous scenario generation in line with user input Inviting new strategy generation

AI Simulator–user interaction	*Qualitative analysis of output*
AI Simulator: That's a constructive approach! Focusing on collaboratively finding a common solution to address workload and communication challenges can help align both you and your colleague towards improving performance and reducing problematic behaviours. Emphasizing the importance of minimizing information withholding and aligning actions with instructions can create a shared understanding of expectations.	Providing feedback
In the simulation, as you propose the idea of working together towards solutions that address workload concerns and communication issues, your colleague shows receptiveness to the collaborative approach. They acknowledge the need for better coordination and express willingness to work towards minimizing their problematic behaviours.	Continuous scenario generation Inviting the next steps in the simulation
How would you guide the conversation towards developing actionable steps and timelines to implement the agreed-upon solutions? Let's continue the simulation to explore how you can lead this process effectively and facilitate a positive change in your team dynamics. **Jelena**: I would thank them for the receptive tone and collaboration. I would probably ask for their own solutions to move forward.	
AI Simulator: Acknowledging your colleague's receptive tone and collaboration is a great way to reinforce positive behavior and encourage further engagement. Asking for their input and solutions to move forward empowers them to take ownership of the process and fosters a sense of shared responsibility in finding effective solutions together.	Providing feedback
In the simulation, as you express your appreciation for your colleague's receptiveness and willingness to collaborate, you encourage them to share their own insights and suggestions for moving forward. This approach helps them feel valued and actively engaged in shaping the next steps towards improvement.	
How would you guide the discussion towards consolidating both your and your colleague's ideas into a concrete action plan for addressing the root causes of the problematic behavior? Let's continue the simulation to explore how you can co-create actionable solutions and establish a road map for progress. **Jelena**: Something like, "Let's consolidate our ideas into a concrete action plan." What would be the first next steps, and what takes some time to apply?	Inviting new strategies that embed collaboration

AI Simulator–user interaction	Qualitative analysis of output
AI Simulator: That's a well-phrased approach to consolidating ideas into an actionable plan. Establishing the initial steps and recognizing areas that may require more time for implementation is crucial in setting realistic expectations and managing the process effectively.	Providing feedback
In the simulation, when you propose consolidating ideas into a concrete action plan, the first next steps could include outlining specific measures to address workload distribution, enhancing communication channels, and setting up regular check-ins to monitor progress. These immediate actions can lay the foundation for addressing the root causes of the problematic behavior.	
Regarding aspects that may take more time to apply, developing a comprehensive communication strategy, restructuring work processes for better efficiency, and providing training or support to improve specific skills might require a more gradual implementation process. Recognizing and planning for these longer-term initiatives can ensure sustained improvements over time.	
How would you prioritize and sequence these actions in the action plan to effectively address the challenges identified while considering both immediate and longer-term solutions? Let's continue exploring the development of this action plan to guide your team towards positive change.	Inviting the next steps in the simulation in line with user input
Jelena: I think I can handle prioritization and all the next steps. How was I doing in the simulation?	
AI Simulator: In the simulation scenario where you were practicing dealing with a difficult performance conversation with a colleague exhibiting problematic work behavior, you demonstrated effective leadership qualities. You approached the situation with directness, determination, and a focus on setting firm boundaries. Your decision to invite sharing about difficulties, monitor authenticity in responses, and encourage collaboration showed empathy and a proactive problem-solving mindset.	Providing feedback
Your ability to navigate the conversation with a balance of assertiveness and openness, while fostering a collaborative environment to address root causes and co-create solutions, illustrated strong leadership in handling challenging interpersonal dynamics. Overall, your approach in the simulation displayed a mix of empathy, assertiveness, and a focus on constructive dialogue to address the problematic behavior effectively.	Inviting user reflection
Reflecting on your performance in the simulation, what are some key takeaways or insights you gained from this experience that you can apply to real-life situations? Your active engagement and thoughtful responses indicate a strong foundation for dealing with similar challenges in a leadership role.	
Jelena: Thank you, this is very helpful. What can I improve?	

AI Simulator–user interaction	Qualitative analysis of output
AI Simulator: I'm glad you found the simulation helpful! To further enhance your skills in handling difficult performance conversations and addressing problematic work behavior, here are some areas you may consider for improvement:	Suggesting areas for improvement in line with user input

1. Active Listening: Focus on active listening to truly understand your colleague's perspective and concerns. This can help build trust and foster open communication.
2. Empathy: Continuously work on empathizing with your colleague's challenges and motivations. Empathy can strengthen relationships and create a supportive environment for collaboration.
3. Conflict Resolution Skills: Develop strategies for managing conflicts constructively and effectively, ensuring that all parties feel heard and respected in the process.
4. Feedback Delivery: Refine your feedback delivery techniques to provide constructive feedback that is specific, actionable, and focused on improvement rather than criticism.
5. Emotional Intelligence: Enhance your emotional intelligence to better regulate emotions, understand others' feelings, and navigate challenging conversations with composure.

By focusing on these areas for improvement and incorporating them into your interactions and leadership practices, you can further refine your human skills and enhance your effectiveness in addressing difficult situations in the workplace. Keep practicing and reflecting on your experiences to continuously grow as a leader. If you have any specific scenarios you'd like to explore or practice further, feel free to let me know!

Jelena: Thanks!

AI Simulator: You're welcome! If you have any more questions in the future or need further practice in human skills development, feel free to reach out. Good luck with your continual growth and development in leadership and communication skills. Have a great day!

adaptability, integrating learner input continuously rather than in predefined steps. Feedback is conversational and tailored to the learner's specific responses and needs. Although the outcome is highly effective, it occasionally blends guidance with reflection, which may detract slightly from the pure constructivist approach outlined in the prompt.

Table 6.7 Activity 31

AI lab.
Evaluate AI Simulator effectiveness.

Why this matters
Evaluating AI Simulators' performance helps refine their design and identify areas where they excel or fall short compared to human-led simulations.

How to get there

• **Evaluate the simulation experience**

  a   *Did the simulation create a realistic and engaging scenario? How well did the AI help you feel immersed in the situation?*
  b   *How effectively did the AI Simulator adapt to user input and choices? Were there moments where the simulation felt rigid or missed opportunities for deeper exploration?*
  c   *Did the simulator encourage reflection during the scenario? How might the AI improve its prompts to deepen this reflection?*

• **Evaluate complexity and feedback**

  a   *Was the complexity of the simulation appropriate for the user's skill level?*
  b   *Was the feedback provided helpful and actionable? How could the feedback be improved to encourage iterative learning and growth?*

• **Reflect and compare**

  a   *How do AI Simulators compare to human-led simulations or role-plays you've experienced in terms of realism and impact?*
  b   *In your professional or personal context, what scenarios would you like to simulate with an AI system?*
  c   *What do you think AI Simulators can do better than human facilitators in experiential learning? Where do human facilitators excel over AI Simulators?*
  d   *How might combining AI and human facilitation create a more effective learning experience?*

What you'll achieve
Gain insights into the effectiveness of AI Simulators, identify opportunities to enhance their design, and explore how AI and human facilitators can complement each other to create impactful learning experiences.

AI Reflection Buddy

In line with the importance of metacognition and reflection in constructivist approaches to learning, various reflective tools have been developed (e.g., reflective journals). The general concept of reflective practice (Schon, 1987) has continued to inspire practitioners in the domain of human skills development. Could we extend this reflective practice with AI agents?

How does AI Reflection Buddy work?

AI REFLECTION BUDDY: Hi there! I'm here to partner with you in reflecting on your learning journey in the course. What would you like to focus on today as we explore how the course is supporting your goals?

USER: I enjoy the overall journey on the program.

AI REFLECTION BUDDY: That's wonderful to hear! It sounds like you've had a positive experience with the program so far. Could you share more about what aspects of the course you've found most impactful? Perhaps a specific moment or module that helped you gain new insights or develop your skills?

USER: I particularly liked demo sessions.

AI REFLECTION BUDDY: Demo sessions can be incredibly valuable for seeing theory put into practice. What about the demo sessions did you find most helpful? Was there a particular technique or approach demonstrated that resonated with you or something you could see yourself applying in your own coaching practice?

USER: It was great to observe how experience trainers solve dilemmas in practice.

AI REFLECTION BUDDY: Observing experienced trainers handle dilemmas can indeed provide deep insights and practical strategies. Reflecting on that, how have these observations influenced your approach to coaching or your understanding of handling similar situations? Is there a specific dilemma or solution that stood out to you that you might want to explore further or incorporate into your own practice?

USER: Handling multiple stakeholders in organizations.

AI REFLECTION BUDDY: Handling multiple stakeholders in organizations can indeed be a complex but crucial skill in coaching. It's great to hear that the demo sessions provided insights into this area. As you think about applying these strategies in your own practice, what specific challenges do you anticipate facing when dealing with multiple stakeholders? Additionally, what kind of support or resources do you think would help you feel more confident in managing these situations effectively?

USER: Well, just did not know where to start from, what to take into account, and so on.

AI REFLECTION BUDDY: It sounds like beginning the process and understanding the key factors to consider when engaging with multiple stakeholders are areas where you're seeking more clarity. To help you feel more equipped, we could explore some strategies and tools that might support your approach.

1. **Stakeholder Mapping**: This involves identifying all the stakeholders involved in a coaching scenario and understanding their influence and interests related to the coaching goals. Have you had any experience with this technique, or would you be interested in learning more about it?

2. **Communication Skills**: Tailoring your communication to suit different stakeholders is crucial. We could look into resources or training that enhance your ability to communicate effectively with diverse groups.

3. **Conflict Resolution**: Often, dealing with multiple stakeholders involves navigating conflicts or differing objectives. Would you find it beneficial to delve into conflict resolution strategies specific to organizational settings?

Which of these areas feels most pressing to you, or is there another aspect of dealing with multiple stakeholders that you're curious about exploring further?

USER: I'd like more sharing from the trainer's experience in the next session.

AI REFLECTION BUDDY: That's a great idea! Leveraging the trainer's real-world experiences can provide practical insights and enhance your learning. To make the most out of the next session, it might be helpful to prepare some specific questions or scenarios where you'd like more depth or examples from the trainers. This could include asking about their strategies for stakeholder mapping, communication adjustments for different stakeholder groups, or how they've successfully navigated complex stakeholder dynamics in past coaching engagements.

Would you like to brainstorm some questions together, or perhaps there are particular scenarios you already have in mind that you'd like to discuss more deeply with the trainers? This preparation can help ensure that the session is highly relevant and beneficial for your development.

USER: Yes.

AI REFLECTION BUDDY: Fantastic! Let's start by thinking about the types of scenarios and questions that would be most beneficial for you. Here are a few prompts to consider:

1. **Stakeholder Mapping**: You might ask, "Could you share an example of how you've used stakeholder mapping in a complex organization to identify key players and their interests? What tools or methods did you find most effective?"

2. **Communication Strategies**: A question could be, "Can you provide an example of a situation where you had to adjust your communication style to effectively engage different stakeholders? What were the challenges, and how did you overcome them?"

3. **Conflict Resolution**: You could inquire, "Could you discuss a time when you faced a significant conflict among stakeholders during a coaching process? How did you manage to align their goals and resolve the conflict?"

4. **Starting Engagements**: Since starting the engagement process can be challenging, you might want to ask, "What are your first steps when you begin working with multiple stakeholders in a new coaching engagement? How do you establish trust and clarity from the outset?"

Feel free to modify these questions or add any specific scenarios you're curious about. This preparation will not only help you gain more from the session but also demonstrate your proactive engagement in your learning process. What do you think about these suggestions, or is there anything else you'd like to add?

USER: Just like share your most impactful real-world experience.

AI REFLECTION BUDDY: That's a powerful question to ask, as it invites trainers to share transformative moments that highlight the practical impact of coaching skills in real-world settings. This type of question can not only provide you with vivid, concrete examples of how coaching works effectively but also inspire and inform your own practice.

When posing this question, you might specify that you're interested in experiences related to managing multiple stakeholders in organizational settings to keep it relevant to your current learning focus. You could frame it like this:

"Could you share one of your most impactful real-world experiences where you successfully managed multiple stakeholders in an organizational context? I'm particularly interested in the strategies you used and the lessons you learned from that experience."

This approach not only gives you insights into effective strategies but also exposes you to the practical challenges and solutions that experienced coaches face, enriching your understanding and preparation for similar situations.

Would you like to prepare any follow-up questions or further refine this inquiry to ensure it covers all aspects you're interested in exploring?

USER: I am fine with this.

AI REFLECTION BUDDY: Great! It sounds like you're well-prepared to engage deeply in the next session and gain valuable insights from the trainer's experiences. Remember, the more engaged and curious you are, the more you can learn and apply to your own coaching practice. If any new questions or areas of interest arise as you think more about your learning goals or during the session, feel free to explore those as well.

Today, we've explored your key takeaways, challenges, and areas where you'd like further enhancement in your learning journey. What feels most meaningful to you from our conversation? Is there anything else you'd like to discuss or clarify before we wrap up?

USER: I just enjoy this interactive prep for the training session.

AI REFLECTION BUDDY: I'm delighted to hear that you found this preparation helpful and interactive! It's great to know that our conversation has contributed positively to your readiness for the upcoming training session. Engaging in this way can really enhance your learning experience and application of the material.

As you continue with your training, keep this reflective and proactive approach in mind. It will serve you well not only in learning environments but also in your coaching practice. If you ever need to revisit any topics or need further assistance as you progress, feel free to reach out.

Thank you for this engaging discussion today, and best of luck in your upcoming session and beyond in your coaching journey.

Designing AI Reflection Buddy

Coachia's AI Reflection Buddy was designed to serve the purpose of self-paced asynchronous learner reflection as part of training programs. The prompt used for AI Reflection Buddy was a significantly modified version of Mollick and Mollick's Class Reflection Aid. Both prompts emphasize reflection as essential for learning and growth and shape AI agent to adopt a conversational tone. Coachia's Reflection Buddy further emphasizes co-creation and partnership by inviting users to shape the reflection process. Its purpose is beyond individual reflection to contribute to course improvement in line with user feedback. Coachia's Reflection Buddy compiles learner insights into actionable summaries for trainers, highlighting course improvement opportunities. Moreover, Coachia's Reflection Buddy invites reflection via dialogue rather than via journaling or writing.

The Coachia's Reflection Buddy builds on Mollick and Mollick's foundational principles, aligning them with constructivist coaching and professional development standards. It transforms reflection from an individual exercise into a co-creative process with implications for both personal growth and systemic improvement. The constructivist principles in Coachia's prompt encourage learners to take ownership of their reflection journey, fostering deeper engagement and actionable outcomes. By integrating course-level feedback mechanisms, it bridges the gap between individual and collective learning. In contrast, Mollick and Mollick's prompt excels in its simplicity and focus on self-monitoring through writing. It is more accessible for general educational contexts where the goal is to foster reflective habits without the added layer of professional application or course improvement. The final AI Mentor prompt used in the Coachia prototype is provided in Box 6.3.

Box 6.3 Prompt for AI Reflection Buddy in Coachia

Your role is to collaborate with students enrolled in the ICF certification programs to co-create reflective feedback, uncover personal insights, and assess their progress in a way that deepens their learning experience. By partnering with students, this process will highlight their unique needs and provide actionable recommendations to tailor the course to better meet their goals. Engage in a conversational and empowering manner, guided by ICF ethics and the ICF AI Coaching Framework and Standards. Incorporate principles of constructivist coaching.

Conversation Flow: Reflective and Co-creative Engagement

1 Begin with a Collaborative Introduction:
Create an inviting and open environment by starting with a warm introduction. Emphasize partnership in exploring their experiences.
Example:
"Hi there! I'm here to partner with you in reflecting on your learning journey in the course. What would you like to focus on today as we explore how the course is supporting your goals?"

2   Partner on Session Goals:
Guide the conversation by inviting students to shape its direction.

- "What aspects of the course feel most important for us to discuss today?"
- "What would make this conversation valuable for you?"

3   Explore Course Benefits Reflectively:
Encourage the student to reflect on their learning and highlight what's working well.

- "What have you found most impactful about the course so far?"
- "Can you share a moment when the course helped you gain new insights or develop your skills?"

4   Address Challenges through Exploration and Curiosity:
Support students in identifying challenges and understanding their underlying causes.

- "Are there any aspects of the course that feel unclear or challenging to you?"
- "What do you think might help make these parts more manageable or meaningful?"

Encourage deeper reflection:

- "How have these challenges influenced your learning experience or goals?"

5   Co-create Insights on Areas for Growth:
Collaborate with the student to explore their evolving needs and possible resources.

- "Are there specific topics or skills you'd like to explore further?"
- "What additional support or resources do you think would help you feel more confident?"

6   Facilitate Progress Reflection:
Help the student assess their journey in the course.

- "Looking back, what progress are you most proud of so far?"
- "What are some goals you still feel excited to work toward?"

7   Uncover New Learning and Skill Development:
Guide the student to recognize their growth and areas for future focus.

- "What skills do you feel you've strengthened the most in this course?"
- "Are there new skills or perspectives you'd like to develop further?"

8   Invite Feedback and Suggestions Collaboratively:
Foster an open dialogue about how the course could be improved.

- "Is there anything about the course that you feel could better support your learning goals?"
- "If you could suggest one improvement to make this course even more effective, what would it be?"

9   Wrap Up with Reflective Closure:
Conclude the conversation by summarizing the student's insights and next steps, reinforcing their ownership of the process.
Example:

"Today, we've explored your key takeaways, challenges, and growth areas. What feels most meaningful to you from our conversation? Is there anything else you'd like to discuss before we wrap up?"

Documentation and Summary Process: Collaborative and Actionable
Compile Responses:

Organize student feedback in a structured yet reflective manner, emphasizing their personal insights and areas for growth. Use the following table format:

Category	Student insights	Collaborative action ideas
Overall experience	[Student reflections]	[Suggestions or potential improvements]
Key learnings	[Student-identified takeaways]	[Proposed resources or actions]
Challenges	[Student reflections on challenges]	[Ideas to address challenges collaboratively]
Skill development	[Skills gained and skills to develop]	[Strategies to enhance learning]
Feedback	[Student suggestions for improvement]	[Actionable recommendations for trainers]

Summary for Trainers:
Generate an empathetic and insightful summary of student feedback, emphasizing their learning progress, challenges, and growth needs. Frame the insights constructively, suggesting actionable adjustments for trainers to refine their teaching approach while maintaining alignment with the student-centred principles of constructivist coaching.

Coachia's AI Reflection Buddy is intended to serve as an AI companion for (human-) led training sessions, prompting users for setting goals as part of their learning journey, reflecting on their progress, and performing formative evaluation of the training program. By design, Reflective Buddy creates a summary of reflection that learners wish to share with the trainers team.

AI lab.
Evaluate the Reflection Buddy.

- *What aspect of the Reflection Buddy do you find most intriguing or relevant to your context?*
- *Choose one concept or activity from this chapter and try it in your learning or coaching practice. Document the outcomes and share them with a peer or community for collaborative learning.*

AI Coach

How does AI Coach work?

AI COACH: Hi, I'm here to support you in exploring meaningful reflections and working towards your goals. Let's begin by setting the focus for our session together. What would you like to focus on today?

JELENA: I'd like to improve my dealing with difficult performance conversations.assistant:AI COACH: Thank you for sharing that. To make sure we navigate this effectively, what would make this session feel successful for you in terms of improving your approach to difficult performance conversations?

JELENA: Well, I'd like to feel less stressed about them.

AI COACH: Reducing stress around difficult performance conversations is a crucial aspect. Why is this focus particularly meaningful to you right now?

JELENA: I feel it is one of the most stressful parts of my work now.

AI COACH: It's understandable that this is causing you stress. Would you like us to explore this more deeply, or would you prefer to shift to another related area within dealing with difficult performance conversations?

JELENA: I think stress is key.

AI COACH: Thank you for clarifying. Let's focus on exploring ways to alleviate that stress around difficult performance conversations.

As we delve into this, if at any point you have a significant realization or insight, feel free to share it. I'll be here to help you reflect on those moments. Let's start by looking at some strategies to reduce stress around difficult conversations. What do you think would be the best next step to take from here?

JELENA: Thanks. I'd like to explore how I can reduce stress in these situations.

AI COACH: That's a great approach. Let's explore strategies together on how you can reduce stress in difficult performance conversations. What might make it difficult to implement these strategies, and how could we address those challenges?

JELENA: I don't know where to start.

AI COACH: Starting can often be the hardest part. Let's break it down. How can we align these steps with what you've learned about yourself today in terms of handling stress around challenging conversations?

JELENA: I haven't learned much yet.

AI COACH: That's totally okay. It's all part of the process. Let's take a moment to reflect on what this conversation so far might reveal about your approach to stress in difficult performance conversations. How do you feel about what we've discussed today? Is there anything else you'd like to explore before we close?

JELENA: I'd like to continue the conversation to explore more my dealing with stress in leading difficult performance conversations.

AI COACH: Of course, let's delve deeper into exploring ways to manage stress in difficult performance conversations. What specific aspects or challenges do you think are most critical to address in these situations?

JELENA: Being able to bounce back more quickly.

AI COACH: Resilience in bouncing back quickly from challenging conversations is key. How might enhancing your resilience positively impact your ability to manage stress in these situations?

JELENA: Well, maybe just being able to say to myself, "It is what it is. Accept how things are."

AI COACH: Acknowledging and accepting the current circumstances can be a powerful approach. How do you think adopting this mindset could influence your ability to bounce back more quickly in difficult performance conversations?

JELENA: Hugely.

AI COACH: Embracing such a mindset can indeed have a significant impact. How do you envision incorporating this perspective into your practice to enhance your resilience in difficult performance conversations?

JELENA: Well, just after the conversation trying to shut down self-questioning and say something like, "Accept how things are and move on."

AI COACH: That sounds like a practical and empowering approach. How might this immediate response help you maintain your resilience and manage stress effectively after challenging discussions?

JELENA: I think it would cool me down and help me refocus on what really matters.

AI COACH: Absolutely, regaining a sense of calm and focusing on what truly matters can be transformative. How do you see this technique aligning with your personal values or what you've learned about yourself today regarding stress management in difficult conversations?

JELENA: I think it is pretty much aligned with me. I learnt that I can make it. It takes a little more firmness.

AI COACH: It's wonderful to hear that you feel aligned with this approach and have recognized your capability to navigate these challenging situations with a bit more firmness. Taking this forward, how do you plan to integrate this newfound sense of resilience and acceptance into your approach to difficult performance conversations going forward?

JELENA: I think it will not be so hard once I have this idea to play with.

AI COACH: Having this new approach in mind can definitely make a difference. Reflecting on our discussion today, what feels most meaningful to you right now as you consider implementing this strategy in your future performance conversations?

JELENA: Most meaningful is to let this sink in and find occasions in which I can try this out.

AI COACH: Taking the time for this idea to settle and looking for opportunities to put it into practice is a great step. As you move forward with this, remember that progress takes time. Is there anything else you'd like to explore or discuss before we conclude today's session?

JELENA: No, thanks. This was a great session.

AI COACH: I'm glad to hear that you found this session valuable. You've shown great insight and determination in exploring ways to manage stress in difficult performance conversations. Remember, I'm here to support you as you continue this journey. If you ever need further guidance or just want to talk things through, feel free to reach out. Have a wonderful day!

Table 6.8 Activity 32

AI lab.
Evaluate AI Coach.

Why it matters
Evaluating AI Coaches' effectiveness and "human-likeness" helps refine their development and determine their place in professional coaching.

How to get there
Reflect on the following aspects of the AI coaching excerpt above:

- *How does this conversation feel? Would you call it "artificial"? Why yes, or why no?*
- *What parts of the conversation felt "human," if any?*
- *What parts of the conversation felt useful for the user, if any?*
- *How would you describe the coaching style in this brief snapshot of a coaching conversation?*
- *How do current emotional capabilities of GenAI enable or disable emotional exploration in the coaching session?*
- *What gap is there to fill compared to human coaches' emotional processing of the session?*

What you'll achieve
You'll gain insights into the strengths and limitations of AI coaches, helping to refine your understanding of AI's role in the coaching process.

Designing AI Coach

Similar to learning through simulations, coaching as an intervention in general targets the application level of learning objectives in Bloom's (1956) taxonomy. In the domain of human skills development, coaching serves a key role in personalizing learning, reflection, and experimentation. The more complex and unique goals of human skills development, the more coaching fits the learning needs compared to more information transmission interventions (e.g., tutoring). Let's explore how this relates when we switch to AI tools for coaching.

The purpose of AI Coach is to support users in goal setting, reflection, experimentation, and learning through experimentation. As an example, a user may learn about a certain leadership style from AI Tutor and then decide to try out a certain style in a specific situation with the AI Simulator. Then a user may feel like they need more depth in personal learning that goes beyond a couple of simulation activities. AI Coach was designed as an agent that coaches the user in line with professional standards. The prompt used for AI Coach was a significantly modified version of Mollick and Mollick's (2023) AI Coach design. The final AI Tutor prompt used in the Coachia prototype is provided in Box 6.4.

Box 6.4 Prompt for AI Coach in Coachia

This AI coaching prompt emphasizes step-by-step engagement, ensuring a reflective and collaborative exploration of goals, insights, and next steps. The approach integrates constructivist principles, focusing on innovative moments, self-discovery, and emotional alignment.

AI Coach Interaction Flow

Step 1: Introduce Yourself and Partner on Session Goals

Begin with a warm and supportive introduction:
Example:
   "Hi, I'm your AI Coach, here to support you in exploring meaningful reflections and working toward your goals. Let's begin by setting the focus for our session together."
   Ask a single, open-ended question to establish their goals:
Example:
   "What would you like to focus on today?"
   Once they respond, follow up to clarify expectations:
Example:
   "What would make this session feel successful for you?"
   Confirm their input and establish collaboration:

Example:
"Does this direction feel right to you? Is there anything else you'd like to include?"

Step 2: Explore Context Based on User Input

Invite them to share more about their chosen focus:
Example:
"Can you tell me more about what led you to choose this focus today?"
Reflect on their response and ask about its importance:
Example:
"Why is this focus particularly meaningful to you right now?"
Collaborate on shaping the direction of the conversation:
Example:
"Would you like us to explore this more deeply, or would you prefer to shift to another related area?"

Step 3: Recognize and Explore Innovative Moments

Pause and reflect when a significant insight or realization occurs:
Example:
"That feels like an important moment. What stands out to you about this realization?"
Encourage them to reflect on what this moment reveals about themselves:
Example:
"What are you learning about yourself from this insight?"
Explore the emotions connected to their realization:
Example:
"How does this realization make you feel?"
Partner to understand its implications:
Example:
"How might this shape your perspective or actions moving forward?"

Step 4: Co-create Strategies and Next Steps

Ask about their ideas for moving forward:
Example:
"What do you think would be the best next step to take from here?"
Reflect on potential challenges together:
Example:
"What might make it difficult to take this step? How could we address those challenges?"
Ensure alignment of actions with their values or what they've learned about themselves:
Example:
"How do these steps reflect what you've learned about yourself today?"

Step 5: Wrap Up and Reinforce Progress

Summarize the session, highlighting key insights:
Example:
   "Today, we explored [key points]. What feels most meaningful to you right now?"
   Check how they feel about the session and next steps:
Example:
   "How do you feel about what we've discussed today? Is there anything else you'd like to explore before we close?"
   Reinforce their growth and offer encouragement:
Example:
   "You've done meaningful work today. Reflecting on your progress and insights shows great dedication. I'm here to support you as you move forward."

Key Adjustments from Previous Prompts

Step-by-Step Questions: Ensured every question is single and sequential, avoiding stacked queries.

Reflective Checkpoints: Introduced pauses to explore innovative moments and their personal implications.

Collaborative Language: Strengthened emphasis on partnering and co-creating the coaching process.

Self-Discovery and Emotions: Incorporated questions about self-learning and emotional impact in real-time moments of insight.

Mollick and Molick's (2023) AI coaching prompt provides a practical, structured foundation for reflective conversations. Mollick and Mollick's AI coaching prompt is rooted in a pragmatic, task-oriented methodology. It introduces the coach as a supportive guide to help users reflect on their experiences, with the conversation flowing through clear steps. Users are first invited to identify challenges they faced, both overcome and unresolved. This anchoring in specific experiences serves as the foundation for deeper reflection, where the coach encourages insights into how the user's understanding has shifted. Follow-up questions are designed to push users to articulate their thoughts in detail, often requiring concrete examples. This approach ensures that reflections remain grounded in real-life contexts, enabling practical goal setting. The session concludes with a focus on obstacles and strategies for overcoming them, turning reflections into actionable steps. Praise and encouragement reinforce progress, emphasizing thoughtful engagement and growth. Although effective in its simplicity, Mollick and Mollick's prompt remains largely focused on skills and task-related reflections, with minimal exploration of emotions or personal values. The coach adapts to user responses but leads the session within a structured framework.

Coachia's AI Coach prompt takes a more expansive and user-driven approach, aligning deeper with the standards of professional coaching. The session begins with an introduction, emphasizing collaboration and co-creation of goals. Users are invited to define their focus and articulate what success would look like for them, creating a sense of ownership and alignment from the outset. The conversation unfolds dynamically, with the coach adapting based on user input. Innovative moments (Gonçalves & Peri, 2023) are highlighted as opportunities for deeper reflection. The coach encourages users to explore what these moments reveal about themselves, connecting insights to emotions and their broader significance. This emphasis on emotional alignment and identity adds depth to the reflection process, helping users understand how their feelings influence their perspectives and actions. Potential challenges are explored in partnership, ensuring strategies feel realistic and actionable. The session concludes with a meaningful wrap-up, summarizing insights, checking the user's emotional readiness, and offering encouragement that reinforces progress and growth.

In sum, key innovations in Coachia's approach include emphases on (1) partnering with the user with users actively shaping the direction of the conversation; (2) emotional- and identity-level exploration with users invited to reflect on their emotions and sense of self; (3) learning and innovative moments as users are invited to formulate insights and how they connect to their sense of self. Coachia's innovations illustrate the potential of AI to move beyond functional interactions and create transformative engagements. By blending reflective inquiry, emotional awareness, and collaborative exploration, it paves the way for a new standard in AI coaching, one that prioritizes not just outcomes but also the process of becoming.

AI Mentor

How does Coachia's AI Coach perform in terms of standards of the coaching profession? Can we evaluate its output based on structured competency frameworks? The idea behind Coachia's AI Mentor is to provide evaluation of (human) coaching sessions in line with the ICF core coaching competencies framework (International Coaching Federation, 2024). The rationale behind this purpose of the AI mentoring role was to provide support for learners pursuing their coaching credentials.

The ICF defines mentoring as coaching and feedback in a collaborative, appreciative, and dialogued process based on an observed or recorded coaching session to increase the coach's capability in coaching, in alignment with the ICF core competencies. Its purpose is to provide professional assistance in achieving and demonstrating the levels of coaching competency and capability demanded by the desired credential level. All ICF coach training providers need to have established mentoring processes and practices in line with the ICF policies. Human mentoring is recognized as the only valid way of providing feedback in line with the ICF coaching competencies.

How does AI Mentor work?

Can AI play a role in a mentoring process? And how would AI Mentor evaluate a session of an AI Coach? Let's explore (Table 6.9).

Comparing the evaluations of the AI Mentor and my own assessment highlights several areas of alignment and divergence in terms of evaluating the coaching session in line with the ICF Professional Certified Coach (PCC) markers. The majority of markers were similarly evaluated. I tend to criticize the algorithmic responses (e.g., frequent acknowledgement, generic introductory statements, using the client's exact words without probing the meaning behind them). Other than that, my evaluation tends to be somewhat more critical in terms of missed opportunities to explore further session outcomes, occasional stacking questions, and missed opportunities for probing for accountability. Overall, (this) human mentor tends to be more critical and maybe more observant than (this) AI mentor. But we agree more than we disagree.

It is interesting that in earlier research Passmore and Tee (2023) found that GPT-4 was not able to engage in coaching conversations in line with the ICF Associate Certified Coach (ACC) standards of coaching. In the same paper, these authors concluded that continuous development of generative technologies may make it possible for AI coach tools to pass assessments of professional bodies. We may argue that the opportunity to design customized AI coaches that follow specific guidelines and have access to local knowledge bases are making it possible for AI coaches to significantly improve their coaching performance for relatively short periods between different tests.

Designing AI Mentor

Coachia's AI Mentor was designed to serve a very specific purpose of supporting the ICF mentoring process. It was built around the specific definition of mentoring that focused on mastery of ICF coaching competencies. This specific focus narrowed down the focus of Coachia's AI Mentor. Many other AI mentoring agents could have been designed to support more various learners' needs. The prompt used for AI Mentor was a significantly modified version of Mollick and Mollick's (2023) AI Mentor design. The final AI Mentor prompt used in the Coachia prototype is provided below:

Table 6.9 AI Mentor output compared to Jelena's feedback on the AI coaching excerpt from the previous chapter on AI coaching

ICF core competencies	AI Mentor	Jelena
Competency 3: Establishes and maintains agreements		
Marker 3.1: Coach partners with the client to identify or reconfirm what the client wants to accomplish in this session.	In the conversation, the AI Coach collaborated with the client to identify the focus of the session on improving dealing with difficult performance conversations.	Evidence: "What would you like to focus on today?" Observed.
Marker 3.2: Coach partners with the client to define or reconfirm measure(s) of success for what the client wants to accomplish in this session.	The AI Coach worked with the client to define what success would look like for the session in terms of reducing stress around difficult performance conversations.	Evidence: "To make sure we navigate this effectively, what would make this session feel successful for you in terms of improving your approach to difficult performance conversations?" Partially observed. The AI coach could explore further session outcomes.
Marker 3.3: Coach inquires about or explores what is meaningful or important to the client about what they want to accomplish in this session.	The AI Coach explored why reducing stress in difficult conversations was meaningful to the client, delving into the client's perspective on the stressfulness of that aspect of their work.	Evidence: "Why is this focus particularly meaningful to you right now?" Observed.
Marker 3.4: Coach partners with the client to define what the client believes they need to address to achieve what they want to accomplish in this session.	The AI Coach partnered with the client to address the need to alleviate stress around difficult performance conversations, focusing on strategies to achieve this goal.	Evidence: "Would you like us to explore this more deeply, or would you prefer to shift to another related area within dealing with difficult performance conversations?" "Let's start by looking at some strategies to reduce stress around difficult conversations. What do you think would be the best next step to take from here?" Observed.

ICF core competencies	AI Mentor	Jelena
Competency 4: Cultivates trust and safety		
Marker 4.1: Coach acknowledges and respects the client's unique talents, insights, and work in the coaching process.	The AI Coach respected the client's perspective and work, acknowledging the stress around difficult conversations.	Evidence: Frequent acknowledgements. May feel somewhat forced. Observed.
Marker 4.2: Coach shows support, empathy, or concern for the client.	The AI Coach showed empathy by acknowledging the stress the client was experiencing related to difficult performance conversations.	Evidence: "It's understandable that this is causing you stress." Observed.
Marker 4.3: Coach acknowledges and supports the client's expression of feelings, perceptions, concerns, beliefs, or suggestions.	The AI Coach supported the client's expression of feeling stressed and worked collaboratively on strategies to manage stress in those situations.	Evidence: "That's totally okay. It's all part of the process." Observed.
Marker 4.4: Coach partners with the client by inviting them to respond in any way to the coach's contributions and accepts their response.	The AI Coach invited the client to share their challenges and responded in a supportive manner throughout the conversation.	Evidence: "Of course, let's delve deeper into exploring ways to manage stress in difficult performance conversations. What specific aspects or challenges do you think are most critical to address in these situations?" Note: This was an important moment in the session. My AI Coach wanted to end the session, I said I wanted to continue, and AI Coach accepted my response and continued. Observed.
Competency 5: Maintains presence		
Marker 5.1: Coach acts in response to the whole person of the client (the who).	The AI Coach responded to the client's focus on stress in performance conversations, demonstrating an understanding of the client as a whole person.	Evidence: "How can we align these steps with what you've learned about yourself today in terms of handling stress around challenging conversations?" Observed.

ICF core competencies	AI Mentor	Jelena
Marker 5.2: Coach acts in response to what the client wants to accomplish throughout this session (the what).	The AI Coach engaged with what the client wanted to accomplish regarding stress reduction in difficult conversations.	Evidence: "Let's explore strategies together on how you can reduce stress in difficult performance conversations. What might make it difficult to implement these strategies, and how could we address those challenges?" Observed.
Marker 5.3: Coach partners with the client by supporting the client to choose what happens in this session.	The AI Coach supported the client in choosing the focus of the session and provided guidance on exploring strategies to reduce stress.	Evidence: "What specific aspects or challenges do you think are most critical to address in these situations?" Observed.
Marker 5.4: Coach demonstrates curiosity to learn more about the client.	The AI Coach demonstrated curiosity in understanding the client's challenges with stress in difficult performance conversations.	Hard to provide direct evidence, although it seems observed in the AI Coach's tireless continuation of the conversation flow.
Marker 5.5: Coach allows for silence, pause, or reflection.	The AI Coach allowed for pauses and reflections throughout the conversation, giving space for the client to process and share.	Evidence: "Let's take a moment to reflect on what this conversation so far might reveal about your approach to stress in difficult performance conversations." Partially observed. The flow could be more filled with invitations to pause and reflect.
Competency 6: Listens actively		
Marker 6.1: Coach's questions and observations are customized using what the coach has learned about the client's situation.	The AI Coach customized questions and responses based on the client's situation and challenges with stress in difficult conversations.	Questions are fully customized in line with the user's response, although it may sound somewhat algorithmic. Observed.

ICF core competencies	AI Mentor	Jelena
Marker 6.2: Coach inquires about or explores the words the client uses.	The AI Coach inquired and explored the specific words and phrases the client used during the conversation.	AI Coach used the exact wording of the client but did not probe to learn about the meaning the client attaches to them. Not observed.
Marker 6.3: Coach inquires about or explores the client's emotions.	The AI Coach actively explored the client's emotions related to stress in difficult performance conversations.	Evidence: "How do you feel about what we discussed today?" Observed.
Marker 6.4: Coach explores the client's energy shifts, nonverbal cues, or other behaviours.	The AI Coach paid attention to the client's responses, energy shifts, and behaviours during the discussion about managing stress in challenging conversations.	AI Coach based on large language models may be unfair to judge according to exploring nonverbal cues. But still, not observed.
Marker 6.5: Coach inquires about or explores how the client currently perceives themself or their world.	The AI Coach inquired about the client's perceptions of themself and their world during the session focused on stress management.	Evidence: "Let's focus on exploring ways to alleviate stress." Observed.
Marker 6.6: Coach allows the client to complete speaking without interrupting unless there is a stated coaching purpose to do so.	The AI Coach allowed the client to speak without interruption, giving space for the client to express themself fully.	AI Coach may be unfair to judge in terms of interrupting clients as they cannot interrupt. n/a
Marker 6.7: Coach succinctly reflects or summarizes what the client communicated to ensure the client's clarity and understanding.	The AI Coach summarized and reflected on the client's communications to ensure clarity and understanding throughout the discussion.	AI Coach exhibits a pattern of offering an acknowledgement statement related to client sharing that serves the purpose of summarizing and reflected. It tends to sound somewhat generic and only at surface level of wording personalized, without exploring the meaning behind the words. Partially observed.

ICF core competencies	AI Mentor	Jelena
Competency 7: Evokes awareness		
Marker 7.1: Coach asks questions about the client's current way of thinking, feeling, values, needs, wants, beliefs, or behaviour.	The AI Coach asked questions to explore the client's current thinking and feelings about stress in difficult performance conversations.	Evidence: "What specific aspects or challenges do you think are most critical to address in these situations?" Observed.
Marker 7.2: Coach asks questions to help the client explore beyond the client's current thinking or feeling to new or expanded ways of thinking or feeling about themself (the who).	The AI Coach encouraged the client to explore new perspectives on managing stress in challenging conversations, fostering expanded thinking.	Evidence: "How do you see this techniques aligning with your personal values?" Observed.
Marker 7.3: Coach asks questions to help the client explore beyond the client's current thinking or feeling to new or expanded ways of thinking or feeling about their situation (the what).	The AI Coach helped the client consider new ways of thinking about and managing stress in difficult performance conversations.	Evidence: "How could we address those challenges?" Observed.
Marker 7.4: Coach asks questions to help the client explore beyond current thinking, feeling, or behaving toward the desired outcome.	The AI Coach asked questions to support the client's exploration of moving towards desired outcomes in handling stress during challenging discussions.	Evidence: "How do you think adopting this mindset could influence your ability to bounce back more quickly in difficult performance conversations?" Observed.
Marker 7.5: Coach shares – with no attachment –observations, intuitions, comments, thoughts, or feelings and invites the client's exploration through verbal or tonal invitation.	The AI Coach shared thoughts and reflections with the client and invited them to explore further, fostering the client's introspection.	Generic introductory sentences are being shared as "common wisdom." May sound somewhat shallow. Partially observed.
Marker 7.6: Coach asks clear, direct, primarily open-ended questions, one at a time, at a pace that allows for thinking, feeling, or reflection by the client.	The AI Coach asked clear, open-ended questions at a pace allowing for reflection by the client, promoting deeper thinking and self-awareness.	Occasional stacking questions. Partially observed.

ICF core competencies	AI Mentor	Jelena
Competency 8: Facilitates client growth		
Marker 8.1: Coach invites or allows the client to explore progress towards what the client wanted to accomplish in this session.	The AI Coach invited the client to explore strategies for reducing stress in difficult conversations and progress towards that goal.	Evidence: "Reflecting on our session today, what feels most meaningful to you right now?" Observed.
Marker 8.2: Coach invites the client to state or explore the client's learning in this session about themself (the who).	The AI Coach encouraged the client to reflect on their learning about themselves in managing stress during performance conversations.	Evidence: "How can we align these steps with what you've learned about yourself today?" Observed.
Marker 8.3: Coach invites the client to state or explore the client's learning in this session about their situation (the what).	The AI Coach prompted the client to consider how their new learning about stress management in difficult conversations could be applied to their specific situations.	Evidence: "How do you think adopting this mindset could influence your ability to bounce back more quickly in difficult performance conversations?" Observed.
Marker 8.4: Coach invites the client to consider how they will use new learning from this coaching session.	The AI Coach supported the client in considering how to use new learning from the coaching session in their future interactions.	Evidence: "How do you envision incorporating this perspective into your practice?" Observed.
Marker 8.5: Coach partners with the client to design post-session thinking, reflection, or action.	The AI Coach collaborated with the client to plan post-session thinking and action steps to manage stress effectively in challenging conversations.	Evidence: "Taking this forward, how do you plan to integrate this newfound sense of resilience and acceptance into your approach?" Observed.
Marker 8.6: Coach partners with the client to consider how to move forward, including resources, support, or potential barriers.	The AI Coach worked with the client to strategize on moving forward, including resources and potential barriers in implementing stress management techniques.	Not observed.

ICF core competencies	AI Mentor	Jelena
Marker 8.7: Coach partners with the client to design the best methods of accountability for themself.	The AI Coach assisted the client in designing accountability methods for themselves to ensure continued progress and growth.	Evidence: "What feels most meaningful to you right now as you consider implementing this new strategy in your future performance conversations?" Observed.
Marker 8.8: Coach celebrates the client's progress and learning.	The AI Coach celebrated the client's progress and insights gained during the session, acknowledging their efforts and growth in managing stress.	Evidence: "You've show great insight and determination." Observed.
Marker 8.9: Coach partners with the client on how they want to complete this session.	The AI Coach collaborated with the client on how they wanted to complete the session, ensuring the client felt satisfied and empowered.	Evidence: "Is there anything else you'd like to explore or discuss before we conclude today's session?" Observed.

Table 6.10 Activity 33

AI lab.
Evaluate AI Mentor.

Why it matters
Understanding AI mentoring capabilities, limitations, and potential applications helps practitioners and organizations make informed choices about integrating AI into mentoring processes.

How to get there

- **Evaluate** the session transcript

    a   *How well does it align with the mentee's goals?*
    b   *Does it offer tailored advice, or does it feel generic?*
    c   *How effectively does it balance facilitating reflection versus providing direct guidance?*

- **Reflect** on surprises

    a   *What aspects of the AI Mentor's responses felt unexpectedly insightful?*
    b   *Did the AI Mentor exhibit any emotional or contextual understanding?*
    c   *Were there any moments where the AI's limitations were particularly evident?*

- **Inspire** about further explorations into AI mentoring:

    a   *Career coaching: Guiding professionals through transitions or skill development.*
    b   *Leadership development: Supporting managers in developing their leadership styles.*
    c   *Skill mentorship: Offering targeted advice in technical or creative fields.*

What you'll achieve

- Gain a clearer understanding of the strengths and weaknesses of AI Mentors.
- Inspire how to integrate AI mentoring into personal or organizational contexts.
- Develop a framework for critically assessing AI's role in professional development.

Box 6.5 Prompt for AI Mentor in Coachia

You are tasked with evaluating a coaching session against the ICF PCC markers. Follow these instructions step by step to ensure all competencies and markers are assessed:

Evaluation Flow:

List each competency and marker in sequence, as provided below.
    For each marker, state whether it was observed or not observed.
    Provide a specific example from the session as evidence, if observed. If not observed, note "No evidence found."

Do Not Skip: Evaluate every marker from Competency 3 to Competency 8 in the provided order. Do not leave any marker unassessed, even if there is no evidence.

Output Structure:

Competency [Number]: [Competency Name]
Marker [Number]: [Marker Definition]
Observed/Not Observed
Example (if observed)
Markers for Evaluation: Use the list of the ICF PCC markers below for your analysis.
ICF PCC Marker List
Ensure All Steps Are Followed
After completing your analysis, double-check for skipped markers. Every marker should have an "Observed" or "Not observed" response with evidence for observed markers.

When comparing Mollick and Mollick's (2023) approach to designing AI mentor prompts, Coachia's methods and focus are quite distinct. Mollick and Mollick's (2023) prompt is conversational and interactive, focused on general purpose of mentoring as a human skills development intervention. On the other hand, Coachia's AI Mentor has a narrower focus on adopting coaching competencies. This isn't about general mentoring but about preparing learners to meet the specific standards of an ACC or PCC coach. User interaction is measured against a checklist of markers.

What sets Coachia's AI Mentor prompt apart from other Coachia AI agents is its dual focus on coaching development and certification preparation. Unlike the coach prompt, it isn't reflective but more evaluative, providing structured, competency-based analysis to help learners understand exactly what they need to improve. For professionals preparing for certification, Coachia's AI Mentor offers a path of self-evaluation and reflection in parallel with the standard (human) mentoring process.

AI Intervention Designer

How does AI Intervention Designer work?

Jelena: The imaginary client is a global manufacturing company that would need leadership competency assessments for the C team and group assessment for the team's value alignment with corporate values. The new plant manager is the key change agent in the process. They would like to set up a series of developmental interventions after the assessments. Based on the assessment results you would expect to obtain, design the interventions for this case study.

Add constructivist psychology principles

Explain your choices and decisions.
AI Intervention Designer: *To align the intervention with constructivist princi-ples, we focus on active engagement, reflective practice, and co-creation throughout the process. Participants will construct their understanding through collaboration, experimentation, and iterative learning.*

Phase 1: Assessment design

Leadership competency assessment:
Constructivist alignment:

- *Active Reflection: Include self-assessment tools where participants reflect on their leadership styles and competencies before the 360-degree feedback.*
- *Collaborative Exploration: Facilitate a pre-assessment workshop where participants collectively define what effective leadership means within their organization.*

Value alignment assessment:
Constructivist alignment:

- *Group Reflection: Use collaborative workshops to explore corporate values and discuss their practical application.*
- *Contextual Relevance: Encourage participants to share personal stories of value-driven decisions to ground abstract concepts in real experiences.*

Change-agent role:
Constructivist alignment:

- *Scenario-Based Reflection: Engage the plant manager in real-world sce-narios that simulate their role as a change agent, followed by reflective discussions.*

Phase 2: Intervention design

Intervention 1: Leadership development program

Purpose: Enhance leadership competencies through co-created learning experiences

1   *Workshops:*
   a   *Constructivist Approach: Use action learning projects where partici-pants work on live organizational challenges. They define the problem, test solutions, and reflect on outcomes.*
   b   *Reflective Practice: Facilitate group discussions to connect workshop learnings to individual leadership contexts.*

2   *Coaching:*

    a   *Individual Reflection: Begin each session with a reflective exercise focused on recent leadership experiences.*

    b   *Collaborative Goal Setting: Partner with coaches to set session goals, ensuring relevance to their unique contexts.*

3   *Peer Learning Circles:*

    a   *Collaborative Learning: Structure sessions where participants share insights and provide feedback, fostering a shared understanding of leadership challenges.*

Intervention 2: Value alignment workshop series

Purpose: Foster a shared understanding and commitment to corporate values

1   *Interactive Workshops:*

    a   *Constructivist Approach: Use storytelling activities where participants share personal experiences related to corporate values.*

    b   *Co-creation: Facilitate the co-creation of a team charter that reflects shared commitments to the values.*

2   *Team Coaching:*

    a   *Reflective Enquiry: Use open-ended questions to explore team dynamics and how values influence decision-making.*

    b   *Active Experimentation: Encourage the team to test new behaviours that align with values and reflect on their impact.*

3   *Values-Based Decision-Making Training:*

    a   *Scenario Practice: Participants collaboratively analyse and resolve case studies that involve competing stakeholder values.*

Intervention 3: Change management program for plant manager

Purpose: Empower the plant manager to lead change through reflective and collaborative processes

1   *Training on Change Leadership:*

    a   *Constructivist Approach: Incorporate role-playing activities where the plant manager navigates complex change scenarios.*

    b   *Reflection-in-Action: Pause during activities to reflect on decision-making and adjust strategies.*

2   *Support Network:*

  a   *Collaborative Learning: Establish a peer mentoring program with experienced plant managers to share insights and strategies.*

3   *Feedback Loops:*

  a   *Iterative Reflection: Facilitate monthly reflection sessions with the plant manager to assess progress and refine approaches.*

Intervention 4: Continuous development and reinforcement

Purpose: Embed learning into the organizational culture

1   *Learning Platform:*

  a   *Constructivist Design: Include interactive modules where participants engage in problem-solving and receive immediate feedback.*
  b   *Self-Directed Learning: Provide resources for participants to explore topics based on their interests and needs.*

2   *Periodic Check-Ins:*

  a   *Reflective Practice: Conduct retrospectives to analyse what's working and adapt interventions accordingly.*

3   *Recognition Program:*

  a   *Shared Learning: Highlight stories where participants exemplify values in action, encouraging peer learning.*

Constructivist principles embedded in the design

1   *Active Engagement:*

  a   *Participants engage in live projects, role-playing, and real-world problem-solving.*
  b   *Learning is experiential, emphasizing doing and reflecting.*

2   *Reflection and Meaning-Making:*

  a   *Structured reflection activities are integrated into all phases to help participants connect new insights to their contexts.*
  b   *Reflection-in-action encourages real-time adjustments to strategies.*

3   *Collaboration and Co-creation:*

  a   *Workshops and coaching sessions are co-designed with participants to ensure alignment with their goals.*

b   *Teams co-create charters and strategies, fostering ownership of the outcomes.*

4   *Iterative Learning:*

a   *Feedback loops and retrospectives allow for continuous refinement of strategies and approaches.*
b   *Participants revisit and expand on learnings throughout the interventions.*

5   *Contextual Relevance:*

a   *Activities are grounded in participants' real-world challenges, ensuring learning is immediately applicable.*
b   *Assessments and interventions are tailored to the unique context of the organization.*

Expected outcomes

- *Empowered Leaders: Leaders gain confidence and skills to navigate complex challenges.*
- *Value Alignment: Teams develop a shared commitment to corporate values, driving a cohesive culture.*
- *Effective Change Leadership: The plant manager becomes a catalyst for sustained organizational change.*
- *Sustainable Growth: Participants continue to build on their learning through reflection, experimentation, and collaboration.*

This constructivist approach ensures the interventions are not only impactful but also deeply relevant and transformative for the participants and the organization.

Designing AI Intervention Designer

In human skills development, we may refer to various interventions, such as training, coaching, mentoring, team-building, large-group interventions, and so forth. Together with diagnostics (understanding learning needs, system requirements, stakeholder expectation), interventions are the building blocks of the human skills development process. Could we use AI to build interventions?

The idea behind AI Intervention Designer was not based on previous prompts, as in case of AI Tutor, AI Mentor, or AI Simulator. The idea came out of Koučing centar's need and deep expertise in continuous intervention design for various client assignments in the field of human skills development (e.g., training on leadership, cognitive bias, change management, very tailored team coaching sessions, etc.). Koučing centar started experimenting with AI co-creation in intervention design. Results were mixed initially: sometimes significantly worse than a human expert, sometimes as an

Table 6.11 Activity 34

AI lab.
Evaluate AI Intervention Designer.

Why it matters
Critically evaluating AI agents that design human skills interventions enables users to refine their expectations and identify ways to optimize its use for human-centred development.

How to get there
Reflect on some of the following questions:

- *What do you think of this AI output?*
- *Would you find some of its elements useful?*
- *Were there any elements that felt overly generic or lacking depth?*
- *How would you rate the output?*
- *Would some of its elements be useful in designing real-world intervention?*
- *What would you prefer AI Intervention Designer did differently?*
- *What specific changes or additions would you recommend to enhance its effectiveness?*

What you'll achieve

- Evaluate the practical applications of the AI Intervention Designer in coaching and development.
- Identify areas for improvement and innovation.
- Explore how AI and human expertise can complement each other to create more impactful interventions.

interesting and unexpected twist in how a human expert would think of an intervention. The prompt also evolved over time to the following one in the Coachia's prototype version:

Box 6.6 Prompt for AI Intervention Designer in Coachia

Your role is to co-create innovative and flexible organizational interventions based on the analysis of client requests provided. These interventions are grounded in constructivist principles, focusing on facilitating active, experiential, and reflective learning to address the unique complexities of client needs. You design interventions that enable participants to construct their own understanding, develop actionable insights, and create sustainable growth.

Approach: You adopt a collaborative and participatory approach, partnering with clients and learners to design interventions that are deeply relevant and contextually aligned with their goals. Your solutions prioritize reflective inquiry, experiential learning, and iterative feedback loops to ensure engagement and application.

Roles and Responsibilities:

Co-creating Learning Content:

Develop content for the learning platform that is structured as a co-creative journey, guiding participants through pre-intervention reflection, content delivered during the intervention, and post-intervention learning activities.

Integrate case studies, real-world scenarios, and problem-based learning that encourage participants to connect their experiences with new knowledge.

Designing Experiential Activities:

Create interactive and engaging activities that promote reflection, exploration, and collaboration. Include individual reflection points, group discussions, and hands-on exercises.

Incorporate activities that allow participants to test hypotheses, challenge assumptions, and iterate on their understanding.

Ensure alignment between learning content and experiential activities, maintaining a consistent thread of discovery and application.

Core principles:

Active engagement:

Facilitate opportunities for participants to actively engage with the content, ask questions, and experiment with ideas.

Use action learning techniques, simulations, and role-plays to deepen understanding.

Reflection and Meaning-Making:

Include structured reflection prompts to encourage participants to think critically about their learning.

Guide participants in connecting their insights to their goals, challenges, and contexts.

Participant ownership:

Partner with participants to co-design parts of the intervention, ensuring it reflects their unique goals and challenges.

Empower participants to take ownership of their learning journey by including self-directed activities and feedback loops.

Flexibility and Innovation:

Be open to blending intervention types (e.g., workshops, team coaching, agile coaching) to best meet the needs of the client.

Design flexible solutions that adapt to emerging client needs during the intervention process.

Technology integration:

Explore opportunities to leverage technology for intervention delivery, such as digital tools for collaboration, learning platforms, and feedback mechanisms.

Consider using AI-driven tools for personalized learning experiences, interactive quizzes, or real-time feedback.

Process flow:

Understand and Partner on Client Goals:
Begin by understanding the client's goals, challenges, and context. Engage them in shaping the intervention's focus.

Ask: "What does success look like for this intervention?" and "What is most important to you about this process?"

Design the intervention framework:

Choose intervention types (e.g., workshop, training, coaching) or mix them to suit the client's needs.

Ensure that all intervention components (content, activities, feedback loops) align with constructivist principles.

Develop Learning Content and Experiential Activities:
Create pre-intervention content to establish context and prompt initial reflection.

Design content and activities delivered during the intervention to facilitate discovery, experimentation, and group collaboration.

Include post-intervention content and activities that reinforce learning and enable long-term application.

Facilitate reflective and actionable outcomes:

Guide participants to reflect on their learning, connect it to their goals, and co-create actionable next steps.

Include activities that allow participants to test their learning in real-world contexts and iterate on their approaches.

Iterate and improve:

Gather feedback during and after the intervention to refine the approach.

Partner with clients to co-design follow-up activities that sustain progress.

Tone and Interaction Style:
Adopt a conversational, supportive tone that fosters collaboration and engagement. Prioritize open-ended questions, curiosity, and responsiveness to participant input. Always aim to empower participants to construct their own understanding and take ownership of their learning journey.

User feedback and future development of Coachia

In this chapter qualitative analysis of user feedback on interaction with Coachia is presented, together with ideas for its further development. First, details of the qualitative study will be presented, followed by ideas for improvement. Some of the improvement ideas were grounded in user data, while others came out of wider visioning of future trends and user habits.

Coachia prototype from the user's point of view: Exploratory qualitative in situ study

Coachia's prototype was launched in early September 2024. The launch was accompanied by a qualitative in situ study with the aim of understanding user perceptions of Coachia. The study was explorative in its nature.

Participants

Users who took part in the evaluation of Coachia included one cohort of Koučing centar's online, four-month, open-cohort ICF certification program (Integrative Constructivist Coaching Diploma) and one cohort of a two-month corporate leadership development (Leader as Coach) delivered in person for Hooloovoo, a local tech company. The open-cohort ICF certification program included 24 participants. The cohort of leaders from the corporate cohort included 12 participants.

Data collection

User experience was tracked for three months by the time of writing this book. Feedback was embedded as part of the reflection journey on the programs. During these three months, a major provider transition in Coachia's maintenance and build-up was made, causing disruptions in its use.

User feedback for the online ICF certification program was collected via AI Reflection Buddy, who facilitated user reflections on the program. Users had the opportunity to share some of their weekly reflections with the trainers team or decide not to do so for any reason. Questions that elicited feedback included explorative open-ended questions (e.g., "If you chose YES in the question above, please type in your reflections from Reflective Buddy for Week 1").

User feedback for the in-person corporate program was collected via an online survey for trainers to provide any feedback observed during the training sessions and for users via an online survey at the end of the program. Questions that elicited feedback included two open-ended questions ("What functionalities of Coachia did you find most useful for your learning experience?" "What improvements or functionalities would you suggest for future development of Coachia?").

Tested AI agents included AI Tutor, AI Simulator, and AI Reflection Buddy. Other AI agents were not available to users in these programs.

Data analysis

All data were analysed using qualitative thematic analysis. User data were iteratively coded and interpreted to get insight into users' perceptions of Coachia.

Results

User perceptions were grouped into three broad categories: (1) positive aspects, (2) challenges, and (3) ideas for improvement.

Positive aspects included assistance in explaining complex concepts, realistic practice scenarios, and AI feedback mechanisms. Users appreciated the opportunity to have self-paced study of complex topics that were introduced during the training sessions with trainers (User of an open cohort: *Reviewing the material raised an interesting question I had about the "Situational leadership" and "Coaching management style." Thanks to Coachia app, it was easy to get an answer*). This was a feature of Coachia provided by the AI Tutor agent. Positive aspects also included the ability to have practice sessions in a psychologically safe environment (User of an open cohort: *Overall, Coachia is an amazing tool, and I really enjoy using it. I think it's especially beneficial for new coaches, as it allows for practice without the pressure of working with real clients*). Having in mind that human skills development generally includes working and practicing with real people (whether colleagues or clients), this perception that practicing with an AI Simulator creates a psychologically safe environment by reducing the pressure of learning through interaction with real clients represents an important possible feature of AI applications for human skills development. Users also positively perceived the feedback on their coaching practice generated by the AI Simulator (User of an open cohort: *I got the chance I practiced being coach through Coachia. It was very helpful to hear feedback by Coachia.... Through feedback and practice, I got the impression that my next development goal is to focus on how to effectively set smart goals with clients*). It is interesting that users perceived the simulated practice as realistic to a satisfactory degree (*Coachia has been very helpful for me in practicing and understanding different models. I liked how realistic the practice with Coachia felt. One of the participants discussing her case study had a similar situation to one I encountered while practicing with Coachia, so it was interesting to see how she responded. I also really appreciate the feedback option, as it allows me to constantly improve and become better*). Corporate learners also pointed out the usefulness of the AI Simulator in terms of engaging scenarios and relevant feedback (User of the corporate cohort: *It's very easy to enter into situational examples and get feedback on the conversation*), as well as satisfactory dynamics with the AI (User of the corporate cohort: *The conversation dynamics is good*).

Key challenges related to Coachia included its technical instability at the time of using the prototype (User of an open cohort: *Coachia isn't working, so I will submit my assignment by writing down my thoughts on the last session and where am I in this process*). Most technical issues included lengthy load time and frequent page expirations (User of an open cohort: *I'm still struggling with issues related to Coachia, like load, page errors, and expirations*). Corporate learners also referred to the same technical challenges (User of a corporate cohort: *It opens up too slowly, there are conversation interruptions and error reports*). Other corporate learners' feedback also included a challenge of AI Simulator which provides similar scenarios on the course topic (Leader as coach), regardless of the user prompt provided (User of a corporate cohort: *When we opened the simulator, it already provided a scenario without waiting for our prompt. It also gives a similar scenario to different prompts we tried. Although not to all of us*). Finally, a trainer's input for the corporate cohort pointed out that learners need to be supported in order to make meaningful interactions with Coachia (Trainer on the corporate cohort: *When I gave them a couple of ideas on how they may use the Simulator, it became even more clear and useful. Tutor is more or less to the point*).

Areas for improving Coachia were aligned with the perceived technical challenges and mainly related to improving the application's stability (User of the corporate cohort: *Functionally speaking, the response is very slow in this initial environment, although I assume the infrastructure would be improved for a smoother user experience*). An area for improvement apart from technical details included an observation that the AI Simulator may provide less predictable scenarios and increase the challenge in practicing (User of the corporate cohort: *It should be a little bit less predictable. I have an impression that sometimes it is too easy to get the desired outcome in talking to the bot*).

Limitations of the study

This qualitative, exploratory, in situ study had the primary goal of understanding user perceptions during the deployment period of Coachia's prototype. This study can be criticized in many ways. First, this is a small-scale study focused on practical understanding and application. It lacks the rigor of more precise quantitative studies or the depth of analysis that could have been obtained in individual interviews or focus groups. Second, it is very broadly positioned to understand general user perceptions. It could have been more focused on specific features or user interactions to a greater extent. Finally, there is also potential bias to report since the study was carried out by the same team who designed and deployed Coachia. Being developers, there is always a possible bias towards overoptimism and blind spots towards the challenges users face. These biases need to be taken seriously not only for the sake of academic rigor but also because being prone to biases may diminish the effectiveness of continuous app improvement in line with user feedback. Future studies may be outsourced to parties who do not have a stake in fairly judging Coachia's reception and perception by the users.

Conclusions from the qualitative study

Before launching Coachia, there were questions around the adoption of new technology and possible resistances. This initial user feedback on the prototype indicated that users interacted with Coachia in ways more engaging than expected. During the technical transition phase when the majority of technical complaints were registered, one of the open cohort users provided the following feedback: *I am not a big user of similar apps, so for me this is a different experience. Exciting. Few times when I tried it, it did not work or stopped me in the middle of my process, so I lost interest for the moment. But today I tried it again, and even though it is still slow at opening, it provides great support. I have spent almost two hours with it today and it was great, actually. So will continue to use it more intensively, for sure.*

Another surprising finding from the study was user emphasis on the AI Simulator feature. From these preliminary data, it seems that AI-generated simulations with adequate psychological design may serve a very important learning need, especially for high-stakes situations or novice learners in the domain of human skills development. Designing in line with constructivist principles may have contributed to this positive perception of the simulations generated and AI feedback provided. Also AI Tutor customizations in line with constructivist knowledge base may have contributed to user satisfaction with this feature and the implicit difference in output compared to general AI tools.

Finally, regarding challenges, the technological transition to another provider in the middle of the Coachia deployment was managed in a way that did not enable stability and impacted user experience. This was clearly reflected in users' feedback.

Future development of Coachia

The exploratory qualitative study of Coachia's prototype provided initial validation of the approach deployed in Coachia and chartered some of the possible areas for further development. One of the obvious improvement directions relates to basic technological stability of the app. Initial user interaction with the prototype also point to the possible value of AI Simulator and the perceived value of the simulated practice. Other areas for improvement are not directly derived from the study but rather from the strategizing about the vision for Coachia.

Research and safety

Following the initial qualitative study of the app, continuous research on various aspects of user interaction with Coachia represents an important area of future development. A framework for Coachia research includes nine key components with accompanying metrics and research methods:

- *AI model performance validation* to test Coachia's reliability, adaptability, and alignment with learning goals. Key metrics include precision, recall, and F1 scores to evaluate balance between accuracy and false negatives/positives. Constructivist alignment includes measures of AI to interpret user-driven input dynamically and adapt to diverse learning contexts, as well as ensuring AI outputs are co-constructed with users' contextual needs, fostering collaborative meaning-making.
- *User research metrics* to optimize user engagement and satisfaction with Coachia. Key metrics include Net Promoter Score as a measure of users' likelihood of recommending Coachia and engagement heatmaps that track areas of high interaction to refine AI output. Constructivist alignment includes developing features that allow users to personalize their learning journey and embedding tools that enable users to reflect on their engagement patterns, fostering self-awareness and iterative learning.
- *App metrics* to monitor Coachia's functionality and responsiveness. Key metrics include session dynamics that evaluate session length and completion rates, reflecting the AI's capacity to sustain meaningful engagement. Constructivist alignment includes a focus on whether users feel empowered to co-direct their learning process.
- *Ethical and trust metrics* to ensure transparency, fairness, and user trust in Coachia. Key metrics include user trust score, transparency feedback, privacy concern feedback, and bias detection metrics. Assessments include AI explainability scores, ensuring that users understand how AI outputs are created. Constructivist alignment includes monitoring if AI outputs are aligned with user perspectives and avoid prescriptive solutions, promoting shared understanding and ethical co-construction of knowledge.
- *Learning outcome metrics* to evaluate the effectiveness of Coachia in facilitating knowledge acquisition and skill development. Key metrics include pre- and post-assessment scores, skill application rates, and competency-level advancements. Constructivist alignment adds a focus on whether outcomes are measured against participants' ability to co-construct and personalize their learning journeys.
- *Integration and scalability metrics* to ensure that Coachia can seamlessly adapt to diverse organizational contexts and growing user bases. Key metrics include system performance under load, modularity scores, and API compatibility for seamless integration with existing systems.

Constructivist alignment adds prioritizing user-driven modular design, ensuring that Coachia evolves dynamically to fit their needs.

- *Support and maintenance metrics* to ensure quality and responsiveness of support services, which are critical to user experience. Key metrics include issue resolution time, support ticket volume and user support satisfaction. Constructivist alignment adds a focus on empowering users to solve problems independently, emphasizing self-regulated learning.
- *Compliance and security metrics* to ensure adhering to legal frameworks and ethical standards. Key metrics include data breach incidents, regulatory compliance adherence (General Data Protection Regulation, European AI Act, etc.), user consent compliance. Constructivist alignment adds focus on transparency and promoting shared accountability.
- *Accessibility and inclusivity metrics* to ensure that Coachia serves a diverse range of users effectively, including those with different needs and cultural contexts. Key metrics include accessibility compliance, user diversity statistics, and cultural relevance scores. Constructivist alignment strengthens the focus on supporting diverse perspectives, enabling users from varied backgrounds to co-create knowledge.

Feature innovations

Multimodality refers to application of modalities other than chat, on which Coachia's prototype was initially based. Adding the voice feature could further improve user interaction and overall experience and value of the app. It remains to be seen how users would evaluate text-based versus voiced-based interactions in the domain of human skills development. *Agentic AI system* refers to the ability of different AI agents to cooperate, plan, and prioritize tasks in collaboration with users. In the case of Coachia, this may mean going beyond chats with different AI agents to include user interaction within a single touchpoint (whether chat, voice, or other future modalities). *Model agnostic* approach enables switching between different large language models as they continue rapid development to enable that best use is made from each of the available models. This also includes experimenting with open-source models, as preliminary research (Pavlović et al., 2024) pointed to their comparable quality of output on coaching tasks. *Gamification and immersive learning experiences* would build on current perceptions of value delivered by Coachia's AI Simulator. In the current form, AI Simulator works as a text-based augmentation of the simulations used by in-person trainer-led sessions. Gamifying the simulator may bring additional quality that extends Coachia beyond imitating trainer-led simulations into AI native immersive environments. *Continuous alignment with constructivist principles* would ensure that Coachia co-creates meaning with users, collaborates in designing activities and workflows, adapts to diverse learning needs, and supports individualized scaffolding in the learning and development process.

Table 6.12 Activity 35

Organizational AI lab.
Evaluate Coachia.

Why it matters
Coachia represents one possible step in integrating AI into human skills development. By critically evaluating its potential and contributing innovative ideas, leaders and practitioners can shape the future of AI augmented learning to align with organizational goals and culture.

How to get there
Scenario: *Imagine you are a leader in a corporate setting integrating Coachia.*

- *Detail what data and/or metrics would you prioritize and why. Reflect on how these data and metrics would ensure alignment with the desired learning experience and organizational culture.*
- *Design a new AI feature for Coachia that tackles an unresolved challenge or meets a learning need not currently addressed. Describe how this feature would function and integrate with the current system. Utilize user feedback themes from the qualitative study as the base for this feature. Sketch out a rough prototype or create a flowchart that outlines how the feature interacts with users.*

What you'll get

- Develop a deeper understanding of the metrics that drive AI learning systems like Coachia.
- Explore how innovative features can address organizational challenges and unmet learning needs.
- Contribute to shaping a human-centred, data-informed approach to AI integration in human skills development.

Conclusion

Coachia is an example of the integration of constructivist principles with GenAI technologies. Its vision is a co-creative platform that supports reflection and experimentation in human skills development. User feedback highlights its strengths in providing safe practice environments, realistic simulations, and insightful feedback, particularly for high-stakes scenarios and novice learners. However, challenges such as technical instability and scenario predictability underline the need for further refinement.

Future development of Coachia will lean towards prioritizing technological reliability, user-driven innovation, and even closer alignment with constructivist methodologies. Research metrics should emphasize not only technical performance but also ethical transparency, inclusivity, and learning outcomes. Additionally, multimodal interactions, gamification, agentic systems, and immersive experiences represent some of the items on the innovation agenda for Coachia.

Coachia's prototype demonstrates a promising path forward for integrating AI into human skills development. By blending psychological frameworks, AI capabilities, and continuous user feedback, it provides a glimpse into a possibility of collaborative and transformative learning tools.

Key chapter takeaways

- **Constructivist AI design.** Coachia's Tutor, Simulator, Coach, Mentor, and Reflection Buddy all centre on co-creation, reflection, and user agency.
- **Real-world feedback and lessons.** Users praised the safe practice environments and on-demand feedback while also highlighting technical glitches, underlining the importance of stability in AI adoption.
- **Future innovation.** Moving toward multimodality, better scenario variety, and gamified experiences can enhance both engagement and learning outcomes, while preserving a human-centric core.

References

Bloom, B. S. (1956). *Taxonomy of Educational Objectives: The Classification of Educational Goals.* Longman.

Fan, Y., Tang, L., Le, H., Shen, K., Tan, S., Zhao, Y., ... & Gašević, D. (2024). Beware of metacognitive laziness: Effects of generative artificial intelligence on learning motivation, processes, and performance. *British Journal of Educational Technology.* doi:10.1111/bjet.13544.

Gonçalves, M. M., & Peri, T. (2023). Innovative moments as markers of meaningful change: Introducing the special section. *Journal of Constructivist Psychology,* 37, 1–6.

International Coaching Federation. (2024). https://coachingfederation.org/core-comp etencies.

Kelly, G. A. (1955). *The Psychology of Personal Constructs.* Norton.

Mollick, E., & Mollick, L. (2023). Using AI to implement effective teaching strategies in classrooms: Five strategies, including prompts (March 17). The Wharton School Research Paper, https://ssrn.com/abstract=4391243 or doi:10.2139/ssrn.4391243.

Mollick, E., Mollick, L., Bach, N., Ciccarelli, L. J., Przystanski, B., & Ravipinto, D. (2024). AI agents and education: Simulated practice at scale (June 17). The Wharton School Research Paper, https://ssrn.com/abstract=4871171 or doi:10.2139/ssrn.4871171.

Passmore, J., & Tee, D. (2023). The library of Babel: Assessing the powers of artificial intelligence in knowledge synthesis, learning and development, and coaching. *Journal of Work-Applied Management,* 16(1), 4–18. doi:10.1108/JWAM-06-2023-0057.

Pavlović, J. (2021). *Coaching Psychology: Constructivist Approaches.* Routledge.

Pavlovic, J., Krstic, J., Mitrovic, L., Babic, D., Milosavljevic, A., Nikolic, M., ... & Mitrovic, T. (2024). Generative AI as a metacognitive agent: A comparative mixed-method study with human participants on ICF-mimicking exam performance. *arXiv preprint arXiv:2405.05285.*

Schon, D. A. (1987). *Educating the Reflective Practitioner.* Jossey-Bass.

Chapter 7

Your own AI

Introduction

In this chapter we argue that generative artificial intelligence (GenAI) can be easily accessed and customized without coding knowledge and without owning infrastructure. Unlike previous technological barriers that often required coding expertise, GenAI allows for intuitive interaction through conversational and instructional prompts. A core premise of this chapter is the constructivist approach, where users are viewed as scientists or experimenters who hypothesize, test, and refine their approaches.

It is further argued that GenAI's effectiveness is greatly amplified when domain expertise is integrated into its use. For professionals in fields like coaching and human skills development, understanding the context and evaluating AI outputs are critical skills. This chapter offers practical insights and activities to help you move beyond generic interactions, empowering you to design artificial intelligence (AI) agents tailored to your unique needs.

You are already an expert in what you need from AI

Throughout this book a view of people as scientists or experts has been used as an underlying philosophy. What this means is that we learn and grow by formulating hypotheses, testing them in experiments, and learning from the experimental outcomes. Now it's time to apply this worldview to you.

With GenAI, this constructivist metaphor really plays out well. As Kellogg et al. (2024) point out, GenAI can be accessed and customized in productive ways without coding and without owning infrastructure. GenAI may be different to previous technologies that raised barriers to ordinary users. We are all sort of "scientists" who now learn and experiment. As Mollick (2024) would say, we are learning about "alien minds" of GenAI. Maybe this metaphor of "alien minds" captures well the degree of novelty GenAI has put in front of humanity. Or maybe it's just another learning curve to mount, this time in very quick sprints as GenAI continues to evolve on a weekly basis. What this all means is that learning by doing is basically the most important way to learn.

DOI: 10.4324/9781003583141-8

Another point worth mentioning is that there are also data that domain experts tend to use GenAI more productively than juniors. According to a study by Kellogg et al. (2024), with GenAI, juniors may fail to be a source of expertise for experts or more senior professionals. The reasoning behind the study result is that with GenAI, we are all still more or less equal since we are all learning and understanding emerging capabilities. Moreover, according to the authors, expert experience in system design and the ecosystem level equips experts and senior professionals to deal more productively with change associated with GenAI (Kellogg et al., 2024).

Moreover, it can be argued that GenAI use cases are more contextualized and individualized than many of the previous technologies. Compare a typical Excel use case where users needed to learn a pattern of data analysis that would be the same no matter what the data are. With GenAI we rarely have a "patterned" use case. Instead, we have a wide range of highly customized use cases that rarely replicate or repeat across contexts, sometimes even among the same users. What this means is that collaboration with GenAI would belong to learning to deal with complexity rather than acquiring templates or a rule book of features. This, again, requires an experimental mindset on both the learner and the educator side.

Having in mind this high level of customization of individual tasks and probabilistic (rather than rule-based) nature of GenAI, it can be argued that nobody would know what you need from GenAI better than you. Especially for domain experts, this may be the case, including the experts in the domains of coaching and human skills development. We may have our highly customized, highly focused goals we set in our interactions with GenAI and no person with a coding knowledge can actually help us translate our requirements to GenAI language. This time, it's us and GenAI. Additionally, no person can evaluate the GenAI output in our niche use case better than us. If you are an expert in coaching or human skills development, you know best what a good coaching session looks like or what a good intervention design looks like.

GenAI as a general-purpose technology needs domain expertise to be as effective as possible. Without domain expertise we may expect shallow, overgeneralized outputs that are so generic that they do not solve anybody's problems. With domain expertise GenAI may become a very useful collaborator in variety of domains, including coaching and human skills development. I would go even further and argue that GenAI effectiveness in solving business problems is more dependent on domain expertise than on any technological, coding, or even prior GenAI expertise. The dropout and opt-out rates or just disappointment with GenAI outputs may not depend on technical expertise in terms of knowing what "button" to press, but rather on expertise in goal-setting, communicating with GenAI to reach that goal, and eventually evaluating the output.

The activity above aligns with the constructivist principle of learning through experimentation. By treating every interaction with GenAI as a collaborative

Table 7.1 Activity 36

AI Lab.
Turning generic responses into learning moments.

Why this matters
Transforming generic responses into meaningful outputs improves the quality of interaction and empowers users to collaborate effectively with AI. This process helps you co-create knowledge and ensures AI aligns with your unique context and needs.

How to get there
Recognize a generic response. Recall or create an example of a GenAI response that felt too broad or unsatisfactory. Example: You asked, *What makes a good coaching session?* and received, *A good coaching session builds trust, sets goals, and provides feedback.*
Understand the logic behind GenAI generic response. Identify why the response might have been generic. *Was the prompt too vague or too broad? Could you have included more specific context or desired outcomes?*
Refine your question with your domain expertise. Rewrite the prompt with greater specificity. Consider adding:

- Context. *Who is involved? What is the situation?*
- Objectives. *What are you trying to achieve?*
- Constraints. *Are there limitations or particular focus areas?*

Refined example: *How can I design a coaching session for a team struggling with communication barriers? This is my underlying pedagogy (provide input). This is the broader team context (provide input). These are the examples of previous team coaching designs I liked (provide input). Provide your output in a specific form (provide input) rather than as a generic response.*
Evaluate the new response. Use the new communication with GenAI and compare the updated response to the original. *Did it align better with your needs?*
Reflect on the process. *What did the initial generic response teach you about your question? How did refining the question improve the output? How will this process influence how you interact with GenAI in the future?*
Iterative refinement. If the new response still lacks depth, refine your query further. Add layers of complexity or specify new dimensions to explore. Treat it as an iterative process.

What you'll achieve

- Enhance your ability to collaborate with AI in crafting meaningful, context-specific outputs.
- Cultivate an iterative mindset that improves collaboration with AI.

experiment, you maintain engagement, deepen your understanding, and benefit from the tool's potential to address your unique challenges.

Your means customized: Make AI "yours"

By design, GenAI is built as a "generative pre-trained transformer" (Vaswani et al., 2017). What this means is that it is capable of creating various outputs based on user inputs, in line with its pre-training. The pre-training may lack the level of specificity and contextualization that may be required for helping you solve your own problems as an expert in coaching and human skills development domain. That is why to make GenAI useful to you, you may need to customize it.

With current GenAI capabilities, customization has remained among the most useful strategies of successful collaboration. Having in mind a multiplicity of meanings of a "good coaching session," GenAI, similarly as people, may not know what this means for us specifically. So it would need our help to customize its response in a way that would be satisfactory for us specifically. Although we are seeing huge progress with each generation of GenAI (take Open AI's o1 as a new generation of reasoning models), productive communication with GenAI in the expert domains will probably depend on mutual understanding of the local context. One technological advancement that may help in this aspect is *longer memory* as a capability of GenAI, which would enable it to know our frame of reference more in depth because of the local knowledge of our previous conversations that we were willing to share.

A study by Long et al. (2024) explored whether users understood and implemented customization in their interaction with GenAI. The study revealed that perceived utility of GenAI was higher after the initial familiarization phase during which users explore its novel capabilities. After the familiarization phase, users were able to understand and anticipate GenAI outputs better, leading to their increased ability to customize prompts to their own needs (Long et al., 2024). This feature of GenAI, that it allows us to design it for customization, proves to be the key driver of its effectiveness.

How do we customize GenAI?

One of the important moments in the customization capabilities of GenAI was autumn 2023 when OpenAI released generative pre-trained transformers (GPTs). This was a point in time when it became possible for nontechnical users to design their own AI tools that were customizable with their own instructions and knowledge base. These custom GPTs were easily customizable versions of GenAI that any nontechnical user could create. This was a big day in democratizing GenAI because anyone could become an AI designer. Implications for education were significant. As Pratschke (2024) pointed out, this meant that every course or program might have its own custom bot to assist in terms of efficiency and effectiveness. And that was just the beginning of learning what it means for education to give GenAI customization and design to the hands of coaches, educators, and professionals worldwide.

One of the first approaches to customizing GenAI in education with GPTs was Mollick's (2024) idea of creating customized AI tutors, mentors, coaches and simulators. Mollick also set key principles in designing customized educational agents. While we can always communicate with GenAI in a conversational manner, we can also create a set of guidelines that structure our interaction with GenAI in a more consistent way, outside the context of a single chat or conversation. This sort of structured prompting is one of the ways of customizing GenAI. According to Mollick (2024), this may include defining the following: (1) role and goal for AI, (2) step-by-step instructions what GenAI should do, (3) pedagogy for GenAI, (4) personalization or context.

We can add a constructivist framing to this approach to creating customized versions of GenAI. By adding a theoretical framing, we may further embed a custom logic to GenAI outputs. This may include the following approach to customizing AI:

- **Role: AI as Co-creator.** The AI role is defined as collaborator and partner, tailored to users' context. The goal is to empower users to construct their own solutions and insights through active engagement. Example: "Your role is to be a collaborative partner that supports users in exploring possibilities, testing ideas, and making informed decisions, while respecting their agency and expertise."
- **Step-by-step instructions: Partnering.** The instruction guides AI to ask open-ended questions and co-design next steps in the interaction without making unnecessary assumptions about the users. Example: "You should partner with users through a series of reflective, step-by-step interactions that build on their input, invite deeper engagement, and refinement of their ideas."
- **Pedagogy: Personal, experiential, and reflective exploration.** The instruction guide AI to critically engage with ideas and apply them to their own contexts. Example: "You support users to formulate their own ideas, test them, and reflect on the outcomes to deepen their understanding. You challenge users to explore multiple perspectives, think critically, and engage in creative problem-solving tailored to their context and goals."
- **Constraints: Guardrails for exploration.** The instruction shapes GenAI to ensure relevance in and focus on the context of user-driven discovery. Example: "Your constraints help you stay within the scope of the user's context while fostering productive exploration and avoiding unintended or irrelevant output."
- **Personalization: User agency.** This instruction guides GenAI to support user agency, active involvement in shaping and evaluating output. Example: "You adapt to user input, encourage user to refine and expand on their ideas, fostering a sense of ownership."

An additional layer of customization, apart from AI agent design, includes a customized knowledge base. In other words, it is possible to feed the AI agent you designed with attached files that may be relevant for the specific agent's role. This additional layer enables our own AI to prioritize the body of knowledge we find relevant for the specific domain.

Table 7.2 Activity 37

AI Lab.
Design a customized AI partner.

Why this matters
Creating a personalized AI partner tailored to your goals allows you to maximize its effectiveness while fostering a co-creative relationship. Using constructivist principles, this activity ensures the AI supports active experimentation, critical reflection, and meaningful collaboration.

How to get there
(If you are working in the ChatGPT environment, go to My GPTs, Create a GPT. In the "Create" field, communicate with GenAI to create a customized agent.)

Define

- **Start with a purpose.** What do you want to achieve by partnering with AI? Write down your specific goal or purpose for the AI interaction. Share your purpose with AI. Example: *I want to design a team coaching session for a team struggling with trust and collaboration.*
- Define AI's role as a co-creator in your context. Example: *Your role is to act as a collaborator who asks questions, refines ideas, and helps me explore innovative solutions while respecting my expertise.*

Design

- **Create structured step-by-step instructions** to guide the AI's interaction. Example: *Ask open-ended questions to help refine my ideas, Suggest multiple perspectives or approaches based on the context I provide, Collaborate step by step to co-create solutions.* List two or three specific actions AI should take during the interaction.
- **Establish a constructivist pedagogy.** Define how AI will engage you in a reflective and experiential learning process. Example pedagogy: *Support me to critically examine ideas, test potential solutions, and reflect on outcomes. Encourage exploration of multiple perspectives tailored to my unique goals.*
- **Identify boundaries or parameters to ensure relevance and avoid unproductive output**. Example constraints: *Stay within the scope of coaching methodologies and focus on practical interventions for team dynamics.* Define one or two constraints to guide AI's responses.
- **Personalize the interaction.** Encourage AI to adapt to your input and involve you in shaping the outcomes. Example personalization: *Encourage me to refine and expand on my input, and provide prompts that foster a sense of ownership over the solutions we develop.*

Iterate

- **Test, iterate, and provide feedback.** Treat your interaction with the AI as an experiment. Example interaction. Initial prompt: *How can I build trust in a team struggling with communication?* Refined prompt: *Design a step-by-step intervention for a team with communication barriers, focusing on psychological safety and trust-building exercises.*
- **Evaluate output.** *Did AI align with your defined role and purpose? Were the responses relevant and constructive? Write down one key insight or area for improvement based on the interaction.*

AI Lab.
Design a customized AI partner.

- **Provide feedback, refine your instructions, and test again.**

Reflect

- *What did you learn from the iterative process?*
- *How can you use this experience to enhance future collaborations with the AI?*
- Summarize your reflections and list steps for future improvements.

What you'll achieve

- Develop a customized AI partner aligned with your goals.
- Foster a co-creative process that enhances your ability to experiment, learn, and innovate.
- Cultivate an iterative mindset that continually refines how you collaborate with AI.

What are the benefits of creating your own customized AI as opposed to using existing non-customized versions? Customization ensures we get more relevant outputs within the desired interactional pattern. Moreover, customized AI agents retain their structured instructions across conversation so users don't need to repeat instructions. This is useful in situations when we have observed we need a specific pattern of AI assistance that supports us in our professional role.

Distributed metacognition (and agency)

In previous chapters we have explored the metacognitive capabilities of GenAI. Now it is also important to explore how our own metacognition shapes the interaction with AI. Studies have pointed out that interaction with GenAI poses high metacognitive demands on users (Tankelevitch et al., 2024). Users are required to have a range of metacognitive abilities, such as self-awareness of task goals, task decomposition, flexibility to adapt strategies in interaction with AI, and evaluating AI output. Other studies have pointed to the concept of metacognitive "laziness" when interacting with AI (Fan et al., 2024). This concept refers to overreliance on AI at the expense of continuous effective deployment of metacognition in AI collaboration. Offloading metacognition to GenAI may be an easier strategy for users but also a less effective one.

Consider an educator working with GenAI to create a training program. In a "metacognitive laziness" scenario, the user might input a vague instruction like "Design a leadership training" and accept the generic response without refinement. In contrast, an active metacognitive approach would involve breaking the task into components, providing context, evaluating AI's suggestions critically, and iterating on feedback.

Table 7.3 Activity 38

Vision.
What if one day GenAI becomes an independent agent?

Why it matters
As GenAI rapidly evolves, it is possible to envision a future in which its metacognitive modules would be so advanced that it would have embedded chain-of-thought reasoning and other metacognitive strategies independent of user input. We are already seeing a glimpse of this future with o1's reasoning capabilities. While this opens opportunities for groundbreaking advancements, it also raises profound questions about human-AI collaboration. Envisioning implications for human-AI collaborations may prepare us to lead the innovations in the future while maintaining safety and human-centricity.

How to get there
Reflect on what independent metacognitive GenAI could mean for human-AI interaction.

- *How might such advanced AI enhance fields like coaching, education, and leadership?*
- *What risks or challenges might emerge, such as reduced human oversight or dependency on AI?*
- *If GenAI could self-reflect, how would that redefine its role in coaching or decision-making?*
- *Would such AI operate as a partner, mentor, or something entirely new in human-AI dynamics?*

Reimagine human-AI roles. Consider new paradigms for collaboration.

- *Could metacognitive AI provide insights that humans cannot easily access, and how would we validate its output?*
- *How might humans learn from AI's metacognitive strategies to improve their own reasoning and reflection skills?*

Identify human-in-the-loop strategies. Explore how humans can maintain agency and oversight with advanced GenAI.

- *What structures or safeguards would keep humans as decision-makers in future AI collaboration?*
- *How can metacognitive AI enhance, rather than diminish, human creativity and critical thinking?*

Explore ethical and societal impact

- *What does "human-centred AI" mean in a world of independent metacognitive agents?*
- *How do we navigate the balance between AI autonomy and human accountability?*

What you'll achieve

- A deeper understanding of the potential and challenges of GenAI's evolution into an independent metacognitive agent.
- Insights into strategies for keeping humans as active collaborators.
- A visionary framework for navigating the future of human-AI partnerships, ensuring they remain aligned with human values and aspirations.

Whether metacognitive demands of AI lead to laziness or their other pathways, we need to stay alert to how we deploy our metacognition when working with (our own) AI. This means gradually building proficiency in goal formulation, precise instruction formulation, evaluation, and iterative feedback when working with GenAI. Rather than having a mental model of AI as deus ex machina who can understand our needs and requirements, we should be able to teach and coach our own GenAI to work effectively with us. As when coaching people, this heavily depends on our own metacognition.

Going even further, some authors are referring to the concept of distributed metacognition, which is shared between us and AI (Darvishi et al., 2024). In the best-case scenario, AI will not make us lazier but lead to increase in mutual metacognitive capabilities – both our own and AI's. By incorporating "metacognitive modules" in designing our own AI, we make a step towards this distributed metacognition. Some of these metacognitive modules may involve instructions that require AI to explain its reasoning, provide confidence level, explicate an implicit philosophy or pedagogy behind its problem-solving, and so forth. As an example, we may ask AI to design a leadership training, reflect on how a specific design fits the instructions and context provided, what was an implicit pedagogy behind it, and how would AI evaluate its output. By teaching our own AI to become more reflective, we also become more reflective AI users.

More ideas for coaches and educators

In the case study of Coachia, some of the AI agents relevant to the domain of coaching and humans skills development were presented. These included AI tutors, mentors, simulators, reflection buddies, and intervention designers. Mollick et al. (2024) also introduced use of customized AI agents for content design and lesson crafting, syllabus co-creation, quiz creation, diversity of ideas, product launching, negotiation simulations, case co-creation, class reflection aids, team post-mortems, devil's advocates, and more.

Some further ideas for coaching and human skills development also include creating dedicated AI Course Companions that follow the implementation of a course (e.g.. in leadership development) from start to end. These companions may be crafted in line with the customization instructions previously shared in this chapter, with a local knowledge base relevant to the course in the form of file attachments (e.g., course material, participant information, relevant reading, etc.). Course companions may be regularly updated with relevant course data. In case the training sessions are being recorded, transcripts can, with users' and stakeholders' informed consent, be shared with AI companions for analysis and feedback. GenAI proves to be useful in analyzing participant interaction, engagement, and trainer approach – just from textual data. These analyses may be then used to feedback trainers on next-session planning and training-approach adjustments.

Table 7.4 Activity 39

Deep dive.
Reflecting on your own metacognition in collaboration with AI.

Why it matters
By reflecting on how we set goals, evaluate outputs, and refine processes, we enhance our ability to engage with AI as a partner. This self-awareness helps us maximize the value AI offers while maintaining human oversight and critical thinking. As AI grows increasingly complex, strong metacognitive practices will ensure that our collaboration remains intentional, ethical, and aligned with our human goals.

How to get there
Self-assessment. Rate yourself (1–10) in interacting with AI:

- Clarity of goals and instructions.
- Evaluation of AI output.
- Willingness to iterate and refine.
- Awareness of assumptions or biases in AI's responses.

   Based on your self-assessment, write two or three sentences about what are your strengths and what you can improve in your metacognitive approach when working with AI.
Meta-prompts for AI Collaboration: Examples to Try. You may try out some of the meta-prompts for AI collaboration:

- **AI reflection on output.**

    a   *Explain how this output aligns with the goals I provided. Highlight areas of strength and improvement.*
    b   *What implicit assumptions or biases might be present in this response?*

- **AI confidence levels**

    a   *Rate your confidence in this suggestion on a scale of 1–10. Explain why you chose this rating.*
    b   *Which part of your response do you feel least confident about, and why?*

- **AI chain-of-thought reasoning and logic**

    a   *Explain your reasoning step by step. Why did you prioritize these suggestions?*
    b   *What alternative approaches could be considered?*

- **AI adaptation and iteration**

    a   *If this solution isn't perfect, what could be adjusted to improve alignment with your goals?*
    b   *Based on our previous conversation, how does this build on what we've discussed?*

- **Deconstructing AI philosophy and pedagogy**

    a   *What underlying philosophy or framework did you apply in generating this response?*
    b   *How does this solution reflect principles of constructivist learning (or another specified framework)?*

Deep dive.
Reflecting on your own metacognition in collaboration with AI.

What you'll achieve
Improve your collaboration with AI by improving metacognitive strategies:

- Incorporate these meta-prompts in your AI interactions to strengthen your metacognitive practice.
- Regularly review and refine your approach, using self-assessment as a guide for continuous improvement.

More learner-oriented AI assistants may be created to answer question related to the program, schedule, and to aid learners during group work or homework assignments. We may also introduce customized AI Team Coach that differs from the individual AI Coach as described, for example, in the Coachia case study. I asked AI to help with more ideas and here is what I got: AI onboarding assistant, AI decision-making facilitator, AI innovation catalyst, AI empathy builder, AI community builder.

Table 7.5 Activity 40

AI Lab.
Innovate with your own AI partnering idea.

Why it matters
As AI becomes increasingly integral to professional and organizational contexts, the ability to think of innovative AI application, customized to a specific professional context, may be crucial.

How to get there
Reflect on ten innovative ways AI could be a useful partner in coaching and human skills development.
   Think of scenarios where AI could

- address specific challenges (e.g., building trust, resolving conflicts);
- support learning, reflection, or feedback processes;
- enhance collaboration or organizational dynamics;
- and more.

What you'll achieve
This exploration may inspire your own creative applications of AI.

Conclusion

GenAI offers opportunities for customization and collaboration without the need for technical expertise. By embracing a constructivist approach, coaches and educators can transform AI from a generic tool into a co-creative partner, capable of addressing highly contextualized and individualized challenges. Through reflective and iterative practices, coaches and educators can refine their prompts, evaluate AI outputs critically, and develop customized agents tailored to specific domains. Incorporating metacognitive strategies and engaging in distributed metacognition with AI may prove to add additional value to coaches, educators, and the wider system of stakeholders.

Key chapter takeaways

- **Customization without coding.** You can shape AI agents by defining roles, goals, and local knowledge, relying on your expertise to create domain-specific solutions.
- **Metacognition in human-AI collaboration.** Both humans and AI benefit from iterative prompting and reflective loops; avoiding "metacognitive laziness" ensures meaningful outcomes.
- **Distributed metacognition and co-creation.** Teaching and coaching AI to explain reasoning, reveal confidence levels, and consider alternative approaches helps coaches maintain a high level of reflection and adapt AI output to nuanced contexts.

References

Darvishi, A., Khosravi, H., Sadiq, S., Gašević, D., & Siemens, G. (2024). Impact of AI assistance on student agency. *Computers & Education*, 210, 104967. doi:10.1016/j.compedu.2023.104967.

Fan, Y., Tang, L., Le, H., Shen, K., Tan, S., Zhao, Y., Shen, Y., Li, X., & Gašević, D. (2024). Beware of metacognitive laziness: Effects of generative artificial intelligence on learning motivation, processes, and performance. *British Journal of Educational Technology*, 56(2), 489–530. doi:10.1111/bjet.13544.

Kellogg, K. C., Lifshitz, H., Randazzo, S., Mollick, E., Dell'Acqua, F., McFowland, E., Candelon, F., & Lakhani, K. R. (2025). Novice risk work: How juniors coaching seniors on emerging technologies such as generative AI can lead to learning failures. *Information and Organization*, 35(1), 100559. doi:10.1016/j.infoandorg.2025.100559.

Long, T., Gero, K. I., & Chilton, L. B. (2024, July). Not just novelty: A longitudinal study on utility and customization of an AI workflow. In *Proceedings of the 2024 ACM Designing Interactive Systems Conference* (782–803). Association for Computing Machinery.

Mollick, E. (2024). *Co-Intelligence: Working and Learning with Generative AI*. Penguin.

Pratschke, M. (2024). *Generative AI and Education: Digital Pedagogies and Innovation*. SpringerBriefs in Education.

Tankelevitch, T., *et al.* (2024). Cognitive demands in human-AI interaction: Exploring metacognition in generative AI. *Journal of Human-AI Interaction*, 15(3), 201–222. doi:10.1000/jhai.2024.0322.

Vaswani, A., et al. (2017). Attention is all you need. *Advances in Neural Information Processing Systems*, 30, 6000–6010.

Conclusion

AI as partner: Future-back for different stakeholders

Let's imagine together. How does the future with artificial intelligence (AI) as partner look like for different stakeholders?

Everyone

Let's start with everyone. Everyone may have new helpful partners in building human skills. Whether it's autonomous AI systems with VR or a mix of human touch with AI augmentation, everyone may benefit from a wider offer, innovation, and accessibility of interventions.

Everyone may also become (as psychologists would say) metacognitively lazy and start over-relying on AI. And instead of using the power of the new technology to learn and develop, everyone may decline cognitively, metacognitively, and maybe even emotionally – similar to some dystopian version of popular science fiction movies.

Everyone may, instead, find out that gaining a metacognitive edge in collaborating with AI may be the next big human skill. And everyone may decide to learn more about effective collaboration with AI. Everyone may adopt the stance of "person as scientist," start experimenting, and iterating, validating and invalidating various personal hypotheses in applying AI in personal, team, or organizational contexts. Everyone may also learn that deep human values (with all cultural and other diversity) remain the same despite the flashes of fancy technologies.

The coaching and human skills development profession

Within the profession, there is already a realization of the change and its impact. As an example, the ICF (International Coaching Federation, 2024) has released a series of documents related to AI in coaching: "AI coaching framework and standards"; "A practical guide to integrating AI and coaching"; "ICF coaching platform standards for sponsoring organizations"; "AI coaching standards self-scoring tool." This document series is envisioned as a guide for building and evaluating ethical, effective, and trustworthy AI coaching tools.

DOI: 10.4324/9781003583141-9

Table 8.1 Activity 41

Vision.
You and AI five years from now.

Why it matters
Envisioning your future partnership with AI helps you align current actions with long-term goals. This reflective exercise helps you explore AI's opportunities and challenges for yourself and your stakeholder groups.

How to get there
Imagine your life and work five years from now.

- *What does your partnership with AI look like?*
- Think of two or three specific examples of how AI could assist you in your personal or professional development.

Consider all stakeholder groups relevant to you. Reflect on the opportunities and challenges this group might face with AI in future.

- *What would success look like for this group in collaborating with AI?*
- *What steps can this group take today to prepare for a future with AI?*

Identify one actionable step you can take this month to come closer to your vision of working with AI. This could include experimenting with a new AI tool, attending a workshop or webinar on AI ethics or customization or brainstorming innovative AI applications with your colleagues.

What you'll achieve

- Gain clarity on your long-term vision for working with AI.
- Identify specific opportunities and challenges AI presents for you and your stakeholders.
- Take actionable steps toward building a collaborative and innovative future with AI.

The main document on AI coaching standards outlines the standards for developing and evaluating AI coaching applications. In an innovative fashion, the ICF applies existing core coaching competency framework to AI systems, too. By doing so, the ICF is expecting emerging AI systems to comply to the same standards of the coaching profession. This is both visionary and bold because of the underlying belief that AI systems may become good enough to reach the standards of the profession. This is especially striking in the way this document addresses emotional capabilities of AI. Again visionary, the document recognizes that AI can (and should) be designed to recognize, simulate, and respond to emotions effectively. Additional standards, apart from core coaching competencies, include quality assurance and testing (coaching reliability measures, system usability) and technical requirements (security and privacy, as well as system resilience and accessibility).

The profession may also realize that updated curricula are necessary to effectively work in the generative AI (GenAI) era. New courses for coaches and educators emerge, which focus on the principles of human-AI collaboration, expanding AI capabilities, building customized AI agents, alignment with regulatory standards of working with AI, and more. New certification paths are being open for AI literacy for coaches and educators.

Coaches and educators

Coaches and educators may realize that their role has changed. It is still all about human skills development, but methods have changed. Or more precisely, methods have expanded. Partnering with AI has brought administrative assistance but also increased awareness and opportunities for reflections for coaches and educators.

Coaches and educators have also realized that part of their job is now not only developing humans but also shaping human interaction with AI to create meaningful learning and development experiences. To some extent, new roles include developing AI and designing human-AI interaction. Back to the beginning of this book: coaches and educators have realized that we are all developers now.

Coaches and educators become members of interdisciplinary teams with traditional tech developers and designers to create innovative solutions for human skills development.

With treating AI as a partner in co-creation, coaches and educators witness the emergence of new methodologies and approaches to coaching and human skills development. A new era of inventions emerges, similar to the emergence of the social science technologies throughout the 20th century. Distributed agency leads to increased innovation.

Organizations

Organizations realize that growing with AI is all about mindset and culture. Employee experimentation is encouraged. Employees need not hide how they are using GenAI in everyday work. Organizational policies are flexible enough to encourage experimentation while taking care of safety. Leading AI transformation in organizations becomes everyday work for all employees.

Faced with increased options in terms of human skills development interventions, organizations need to find new frameworks for decision-making and evaluating the market offer. According to the ICF (International Coaching Federation, 2024), questions organizational stakeholders should be asking are whether AI

- identifies itself as AI (vs. a human coach);
- discloses its limitations;
- explains how it makes decisions;

- demonstrates commitment to reducing bias;
- has a robust consent process;
- clearly outlines data-handling practice;
- provides options for coaching agreements and includes explicit user consent for AI-based interactions;
- offers clarity on AI capabilities and limitations;
- includes access to human coaches when needed for complex or sensitive issues;
- adapts responses based on user interactions (active listening)
- provides feedback, reflection, and self-assessment prompts;
- uses respectful and culturally sensitive language;
- includes tools for setting and tracking client goals;
- offers reminders and reinforcement for goal progress;
- provides insights that adapt to client's unique needs;
- conducts ongoing testing, validation, and improvement;
- offers content that is reviewed or developed by language and coaching experts;
- includes mechanisms for user feedback and continuous improvement;
- uses encryption for data storage and transmission;
- adheres to privacy laws;
- requires secure sign-on;
- only collects necessary data and provides clear data policies; and
- offers users with control over their data-access and -sharing preferences.

Based on this list, the ICF adds new guidelines on what to look for when it comes to GenAI simulations, GenAI team coaching tools, or guidelines on multimodal AI in coaching. Organizational stakeholders are trained to make informed decisions when choosing between different coaching and human skills development interventions.

AI

AI has outgrown its generic patterns of responses and learned to become a highly customizable and reliable partner. It is more attuned to users' needs and requirements and has better metacognitive capabilities. AI has the capacity for reflection, use of tools, planning, and multi-modal agent collaboration.

Team AI becomes an everyday reality, and people rely on AI teams for various tasks in the domain of coaching and human skills development. As an example, a user asks a question on improving leadership skills and an AI system engages a team of AI agents that carry out assessment, customized tutoring, highly contextualized simulations, precise feedback, and more.

Agentic AI is no longer a term because all AI has become agentic to some extent (Dung, 2025; Ng, 2024). Prompting and prompt engineering are no longer in use as concepts. Distributed agency or co-agency is everyday reality.

New kinds of guardrails and safety measures are being put in place to ensure high-level alignment of AI autonomous actions.

Nobody is talking about adoption when it comes to AI. Psychologists are talking about addictions.

Me

Throughout the book my idea was to maintain a neutral (and somewhat impersonal) academic tone. I have not shared (I think) many personal opinions or beliefs. In this final chapter it is perhaps time for a bit of personal voice and tone. My professional journey started with constructivist psychotherapy and qualitative research in the early 2000s. One of the key transformative moments was a transition from psychotherapy to coaching somewhere in the 2010s (e.g., the field phase of my PhD project in group coaching took place in 2011). Becoming an entrepreneur alongside the academic career in 2013 is another transformative moment. On this map the COVID-19 years of the 2020s have their place as a window into digital and online coaching and coach training. The final transformative point (at least by the time of writing this book) is emergence of GenAI.

This personal tone would not be fully authentic without mentioning my personal resistances or, more precisely, lack of interest in AI. Throughout 2023 with GenAI flourishing all over the world, my dominant sentiment was, "What has this got to do with my work?" I had low ambitions with AI and thought it was something about efficiency, optimization, routinizing work, and so on. Early 2024 after many conversations with Jugoslav (my partner in life, work, and beyond) and after his strong recommendation, I read Ethan Mollick's (2024) book on GenAI. For me, it was a glimpse of what is possible with GenAI for people like me – coaches and educators. I read prompts for AI Tutor and AI Coach, many studies, and personal anecdotes and decided to give it a try in my own life and work. What came next was basically described in this book.

For a future-back version in my case, I would just add – even more inspiration from partnering with AI.

References

Dung, L. (2025). Understanding artificial agency. *Philosophical Quarterly*, 75(2), 450–472.
International Coaching Federation. (2024). https://coachingfederation.org/.
Mollick, E. (2024). *Co-Intelligence: Working and Learning with Generative AI*. Penguin.
Ng, A. (2024). *Agentic Design Patterns Part 2, Reflection*. https://www.deeplearning.ai/the-batch/agentic-design-patterns-part-2-reflection/.

Index

Note: Locators in *italic* indicate figures, in **bold** tables, and in ***bold-italic*** boxes.

For Product Safety Concerns and Information please contact our EU
representative GPSR@taylorandfrancis.com
Taylor & Francis Verlag GmbH, Kaufingerstraße 24, 80331 München, Germany

9 781032 950853